The RIB

The RIB

THE RIGID-HULLED INFLATABLE LIFEBOAT

and its Place of Birth
The Atlantic College

DAVID SUTCLIFFE

GRANTA EDITIONS

First published in the United Kingdom by Granta Editions 2010
25–27 High Street, Chesterton, Cambridge CB4 1ND, United Kingdom.

Granta Editions is a wholly owned imprint of Book Production Consultants Ltd

A CIP catalogue record for this book is available from the British Library
ISBN 978 1 85757 101 1 (Hardback)
      978 1 85757 103 5 (Paperback)

Designed by Paul Barrett
Design, editorial and production in association with
Book Production Consultants Ltd, 25–27 High Street, Chesterton,
Cambridge CB4 1ND, United Kingdom
Printed and bound in the United Kingdom by Butler Tanner & Dennis, Frome

Contents

For our son Edward
1968–1993
of whom Desmond Hoare wrote
'my kind of boy'

Foreword

In 1962 an International Sixth-form College was opened in St Donat's Castle in Wales. It was named the Atlantic College, and my husband Desmond was the Founder Headmaster.

He had very firm convictions based on his many years in the Royal Navy that understanding between diverse human beings was nurtured most effectively when they were involved in physical activities, especially when participating in the saving of life. As the College was situated on the edge of the Bristol Channel, where we were told by the local pundits that sailing was far too dangerous, an indestructible unsinkable rescue boat was essential. The first imported rubber boat with a flat floor rapidly proved useless, so Desmond, with his engineering experience, plus the original 50 or so students, energetically and enthusiastically went to work.

So the RIBs, as they are now known, were born of necessity and created with determination by generations of students, aided and encouraged by Desmond.

The final result, the Atlantic 21, was sold to the RNLI for £1.

My personal contribution was the designing of the skin suits which made sea-going possible throughout the year.

Naomi Hoare

Introduction

It was a strange, tumultuous, amazingly creative mixture – an Elizabethan castle; the Bristol Channel; a German Jew who converted to Christianity immediately after the Second World War; an Air Marshal; an Irish Rear-Admiral from the Royal Navy; a former soldier, banker, senior colonial administrator and public servant in the most noble interpretation of that phrase who took over the place's finances at the age of 83, one month before bankruptcy, and handed over to his successor six months after his 93rd birthday; sixth-form students from most of the countries of the Atlantic Alliance and a few more besides – and an idea.

This was the Atlantic College, now known as the United World College of the Atlantic, founded in 1962 in South Wales and the forerunner (in 2010) of 12 sister colleges, with more in the pipeline.

From this school emerged in the 1960s the B-Class Atlantic Inshore Lifeboat, named in honour of its birthplace. Already by August 1993 the Royal National Lifeboat Institution was able to report that this craft, since its introduction into their fleet in 1972, had been launched on service 15,601 times, saved 4,717 lives, and given assistance to a further 2,802 persons. It has also become the prototype for a new range of high-speed boats that are now used worldwide in industry, leisure, racing and the military. They are seen all over the globe.

It was an extraordinary technological achievement for a school. Contemporary safety and insurance arrangements would make it an impossible task for a school today. It all happened just in time.

This is the story.

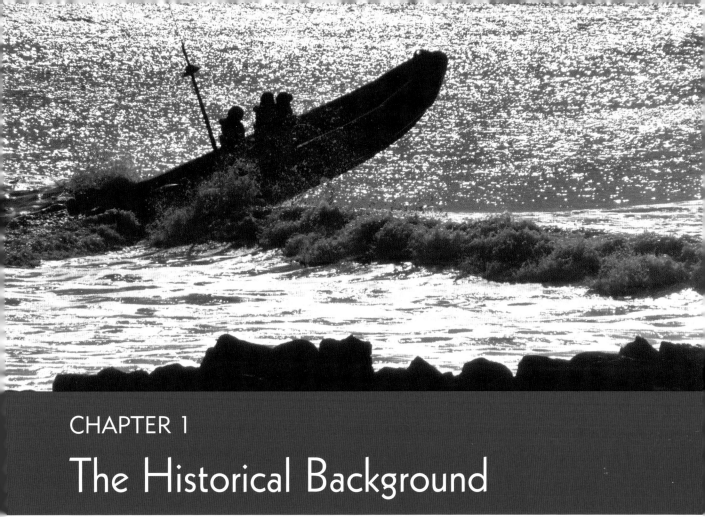

CHAPTER 1
The Historical Background

Most good ideas have some roots in history, however tenuous. The B-Class Atlantic Inshore Lifeboat owes its birthplace to the First World War activities of Kurt Hahn in the German Foreign Office, the educational ideas he drew from them, and the challenges of the East–West confrontation in the 1950s.

The Cold War has become remote. In the 1950s, the possibility of nuclear holocaust threatened to represent the end game for civilisation. Senior diplomats, military leaders and many politicians were too familiar with war to dismiss its likelihood easily. The pressures on the West to stand up for its way of life led to a more rapid integration of Western Europe, in close unity with North America, than could possibly have been foreseen as the Second World War drew to a close.

In peace as in war, human morale is the determining factor – or so the founders of the Atlantic College believed. The leading exponent was Kurt Hahn. The story of the boats begins with this man.

Kurt Hahn was well known in education. His methods are somewhat superficially associated with physical toughness and an obsession with character at the expense of the intellect and the spirit. Born in Berlin into a prosperous and gifted Jewish family, he had suffered sunstroke at the age of 18, with long-term

Kurt Hahn and Desmond Hoare at St Donat's before the College opened.

complications that kept him out of the sun and heated rooms for the rest of his life. They also absolved him from military service in the First World War. Having been a student at Christ Church in Oxford, where his recurrent ill-health prevented him from ever taking examinations, he was recruited into the German Foreign Office in 1914.

His experiences there decisively shaped both his educational principles and his working methods. His detailed interpretations of British political thinking, deduced from a close reading of the British press; his conviction that his political chiefs were gravely deficient in insights into the psychology of the enemy; his despair over the absence of political courage and statesmanship on both sides; his close involvement in a series of international meetings aimed unsuccessfully at bringing the war to an earlier close; his firmly stated opposition to U-Boat warfare and the German occupation of Belgium, both of them disastrous in their impact on Germany's standing in the world; his relentless determination to gain access to the most influential personalities in any given situation; his remarkable skill in drafting memoranda – all these made him a striking but controversial figure. It was he who identified Prince Max of Baden as the one personality on the German side who, despite the accelerating horrors and bitter recriminations of the warfare, retained credibility among the powers of the Entente; he who conspired and manoeuvred Prince Max into the position of Imperial Germany's last Chancellor and who thereby enabled him to negotiate the Armistice.

Was Germany ever really defeated? Militarily there can be no doubt, but the Entente troops did not advance into Germany and the German armies withdrew in good order; public opinion was maliciously manipulated by the military, notably General Ludendorff, to pass the blame to the politicians and the Jews; discord among the Entente powers and accelerating disillusion with Woodrow Wilson and the psychologically clumsy nature of the terms imposed on Germany at Versailles all combined to leave a bitterly resentful and divided German nation in chaos and despair. Hahn allied himself with ultimately forlorn efforts to restore Germany's name, albeit through the assertion of traditional patriotism and conservative leadership rather than – as in retrospect might have been more effective – through the forces of social democracy.

Even as a boy and as a young man, Hahn was sure that his destiny lay in education. In 1920 he opened his first school, Salem, in the fine Cistercian monastery that was the stately home of the man who had been his political chief in the final days of the war, Prince Max of Baden. He knew, and wrote, that the political and social chaos must lead to dictatorship although, like most, he initially underestimated the ruthless brutality of the Nazi threat and even of Hitler himself as late as 1934. His school near Lake Constance in south Germany rapidly became well known in Britain and the United States. Hahn himself became a focal point for anti-Jewish resentment, surviving attempts at assassination. In 1932 he opposed Hitler openly in a letter to all former pupils of Salem. In 1933, after Hitler's accession to power, he spoke out publicly, with remarkable courage and foresight, against the fascist methods of education in both Italy and, by direct and unmistakeable allusion, Germany. In May he was arrested, imprisoned briefly, and forced to abandon his school.

Kurt Hahn.

By July of that year, warned of increasing personal danger, Hahn left Germany for Great Britain where, welcomed by many who had admired his work in Salem, he was to open a new school that very autumn in Scotland. There followed Gordonstoun in Scotland, the Moray County Badge – leading eventually to the Duke of Edinburgh's Award Scheme – Outward Bound, the Trevelyan Scholarships at Oxford and Cambridge, the Medical Commission on Accident Prevention, and the Atlantic College.

The Atlantic College idea was born in the NATO Defence College, then still in Paris. Hahn lectured there in 1955, the invitation generated by an Italian naval officer married to his niece. The Commandant was a British Air Marshal, Sir Lawrance Darvall. Darvall was captivated by the Hahn charisma. Close to retirement, he devoted himself for several intensive years to supporting Hahn's dreams and schemes. The foremost, most ambitious and seemingly unrealistic one was a series of colleges for international secondary-school students aged 16–19. Neither was reticent in his rhetoric, nor was Hahn in the least inhibited in exploiting Darvall's many personal contacts in the senior levels of the NATO hierarchy.

> *If we can plant the germ of new loyalties in mature men* [he was referring to the success of the NATO College with senior officers], *how much deeper are the roots we could sink in the youth of the Atlantic Community if, at their most impressionable period, we could gather them together in residential colleges … The longing for freedom will never be extinguished in human nature. It is stirring in the young behind the Iron Curtain. Ever since Khrushchev admitted in 1956 that murder and massacre were essential elements in the Stalin regime, many young people in Poland and Russia today look towards the West, full of mistrust and also full of hope, asking a question which makes us blush: are you in earnest about the ideals you profess? Who shall give the answer? … I believe the Atlantic College can contribute to the most important task of our generation – the transformation of the Cold War into a hotly contested peaceful contest of the spirit …*

As it happens, Khrushchev had his own ideas on the matter. In February 1956, shortly after Hahn's lecture at the NATO Defence College, he had told the 20th

Desmond Hoare as a naval lieutenant during the Second World War.

Party Congress: '*It appears expedient to support the construction of boarding schools. We should give thought to their name, placing them in suburbs, in holiday resorts, and forest surroundings favourable to health*'. By 1960 there were 322,000 youngsters in Soviet boarding schools. The target for 1965 was 2.5 million.

It was the great good fortune of Hahn's unlikely scheme that he, some years earlier, had come to know and intensely admire an Irish engineering admiral in the Royal Navy, Desmond Hoare.

Idealistic, even romantic in outlook, Desmond Hoare was nonetheless a very practical man. '*If it works, improve it; if it does not, throw it out.*' This simple engineering principle guided all his activities. He had throughout his naval career been fascinated by the challenges and rewards of human leadership. Unusually, he had experimented very pragmatically with Hahn's ideas in the training of naval apprentices before coming under the spell of the man himself. Outward Bound (he preferred the less reverent title Outward Bounding) was as a result taken up by the Royal Navy. He had a strong social conscience too. Posted for six years to the Admiralty in London, and having been brought by Hahn on to the originating committee of the Duke of Edinburgh's Award Scheme, he realised he knew little of youth problems in the cities and began to spend evenings and every weekend with a boys' club in the then tough district of Notting Hill Gate. In 1958 he was asked by Darvall and Hahn to become the founding Headmaster of the Atlantic College. He resigned early from the Navy at the end of 1961, at no little personal sacrifice in terms of pension and family security. An unusual school had gained an extremely unusual headmaster. It was a perfect match.

And then there was the site!

The Castle

St Donat's Castle in the Vale of Glamorgan was up for sale. The price nowadays seems absurd: £65,000 for an Elizabethan castle with central heating and 32 marble bathrooms, 150 acres of land including landscaped Tudor gardens stretching down to the Bristol Channel foreshore, a tithe barn, and a 25-metre (80-feet) open-air swimming pool! But even £65,000 is a lot if you have nothing to start with, and the money was not found until a Frenchman, Antonin Besse, son of the founder and donor of St Antony's College, Oxford, stepped in. The father once wrote that, had he met Kurt Hahn before he gave his money to Oxford, he would have given it all to him. The son was able to make amends handsomely!

And there was romance and legend too.

It is claimed that, as an early Iron Age fort, St Donat's was occupied by Caractacus, a chieftain who was captured and taken to Rome, where he met St Paul and was converted; his daughter, returning to St Donat's, organised the first preaching of the Christian Gospel in Wales. In neighbouring Llantwit Major, the Celtic saint St Illtyd is reputed to have set up Europe's first theological college some 1,400 years ago. When the first moves were being made in 1865 to create a

University in Wales, Dr Nicholl Carne, the owner of the Castle, offered 6 acres of land in Llantwit Major as a site.

In 1925 St Donat's was purchased by Randolph Hearst, the notorious American newspaper boss and role model for Orson Welles' *Citizen Kane*. He had commissioned a lady agent to find him a castle for his film-star mistress Marion Davies and bought it sight unseen by telegraph from aboard ship in mid-Atlantic. It was he, advised by Sir Charles Allom, recently knighted for his redecoration of Buckingham Palace,[1] who installed the bathrooms and swimming pool and much else besides, arousing the attention and ire of the House of Commons for his profligate removal and reconstruction of historic buildings from other parts of the country to embellish the Castle. But when Marion Davies discovered that the near-by Nash Point fog horn kept her awake, he transferred his interest, his money and her to his other grand mansion, San Simeon in California. Edward Thring, the renowned Headmaster of the British public school Uppingham, is remembered for his belief in the educational impact of beautiful buildings and surroundings, which he expressed in somewhat Victorian style: *'Get the wall on your side!'* The founders of the Atlantic College met his challenge magnificently.

The Stradling family, owners of St Donat's from 1298 until 1736, had even larger estates on the facing coastline of Somerset. The visiting and supervision of the Somerset properties must have been something of a challenge. It is recorded,

St Donat's Castle in 1960, the year of its purchase by the College. On the right the Randolph Hearst sea-water swimming pool.

---

1 The compliment was repaid in the early 1960s when the Head Gardener of St Donat's was engaged to manage the gardens of Buckingham Palace.

ABOVE LEFT:
The Stradling Hall as furnished by Randolph Hearst, later the staff Common Room.

ABOVE RIGHT:
The Breakfast Room adjoining the Dining Hall.

for instance, that between December 1472 and January 1473 there had been two wrecks a week on the Nash Sands. Pirates added to the hazards, and one family member, Harry Stradling, captured by pirates, was held for two years in St Malo, his ransom forcing the sale of some of the lands in Somerset and elsewhere. But they were no helpless landlubbers. Sir Edward (1529–1609), who built the first sea wall at the foot of the estate, against which *'the enraged sea foams and roars in such a way that the wild waves … hurl incredibly massive rocks against those well constructed bulwarks, but all in vain',*[2] had been a good friend of seamen such as Francis Drake, Walter Raleigh and Richard Grenville. A later successor, Captain Thomas Stradling, was the naval commander who in 1703 quarrelled with his ship's master, Alexander Selkirk, when engaged *'in warlike manner'* against the French and the Spanish in the south seas. Selkirk left the ship and remained on the island of Tobago, to become the inspiration for Daniel Defoe's *Robinson Crusoe*.

St Donat's Castle, its beauty and its history, were a formative influence in the lives of the College students. No less formative for them, and the essential scenario for the development of the boats, was the Bristol Channel itself – *'y Severn Sea, which forms a most glorious Canal between it and Somerset Shire'*![3]

2 From a reference to a Latin poem by Thomas Leyshon of Neath, now lost but published in Welsh translation in a famous grammar of the Welsh language financed by Sir Edward and printed in 1592.
3 From the description of the engraving of 1740 by Samuel and Nathaniel Buck.

6

The stretch of coast around Nash Point and St Donat's has a fearsome reputation, and the hazards were not only the natural elements. In 1737, after two vessels homeward bound from Virginia were driven ashore under Nash Point, a mob of over 300 assembled each night until the wrecks were stripped bare. Even the hulls were burnt to get at the ironwork. At midnight on 10th December 1806, the *Trelawny*, bound for Jamaica, was driven ashore at Nash Point and, despite its very sturdy construction, smashed to pieces on the rock shelf below the cliff within four hours. The captain was killed by the falling of the mainmast. The mate, pilot and 15 or so others got away in the boats, but 11 lives were lost.

Of many other wrecks[4] probably the most significant was that of the wooden steam packet *Frolic*, a regular trader between Bristol, Carmarthen and Haverfordwest, on the Nash Sands on the night of 16th–17th March 1831. There were no survivors. Of the vessel nothing but small fragments was found, and bodies were being washed ashore over several months. At least 50 are thought to have been on board, among the passengers a General MacLeod, several other high-ranking Army officers, and Pembrokeshire merchants. It was this disaster that led to the building of the two lighthouses on Nash Point. The most recent casualty was the Severn Estuary tanker *Widdale H* that went ashore just below Nash Point in dense fog on 2nd April 1959, the crew scrambling ashore without

Nash Sands Lighthouses.

4   Grahame Farr gives a detailed account in his *Wreck and Rescue in the Bristol Channel*, 1966.

assistance. Large sections of this ship were driven across the College slipway towards Llantwit Major in the coming months and were at times quite a hazard to College sea-going until at least 1965. This overwhelming power of the sea stimulated an early College mini-research project in which boulders on the foreshore were painted and then observed over the following months as they made their way up the coastline towards the Llantwit Major Spit, disappeared out to sea, and re-emerged near Nash Point to recommence their circular journey past St Donat's beach.

The Bristol Channel may be considered as starting at the island of Lundy, some 40 miles to the west, or even beyond, and extending to Bristol 30 miles to the east, its tides running on a further 40 miles up to Gloucester. Over 80 miles long and some 30 metres (100 feet) deep, it is open to the Atlantic Ocean and has the second highest rise and fall of tide, after the Bay of Fundy, in the world. The tidal range at spring can approach 15 metres (35 feet) and the surf runs in to the shore line at between 15 and 20 knots. This rise and fall of water is further strengthened by the response of the Atlantic Ocean to the gravitational forces generated twice daily by the sun and moon, above all the latter. Just as in a domestic bath, when oscillation is set up by movement in the bath water, the water slops highest and more or less rhythmically at each end. The Atlantic Ocean is an enormous bath tub between the Bristol Channel and the Bay of Fundy, some 3 miles deep and 3,000 miles long. A tidal wave 14 metres (40 feet) high passes the

St Donat's Castle, on the coast of Glamorganshire. At the foot of the cliffs the wreck of the Rothsay Steam Packet (1831).

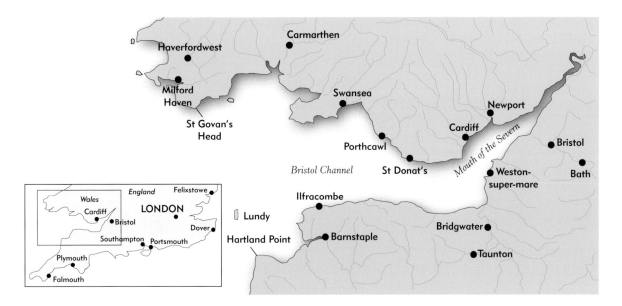

The Bristol Channel.

St Donat's foreshore twice a day in each direction. Thus the Bristol Channel inhales and expels each time some thousand million tons of water.[5] The quantity of water in a 1-mile length of this wave is 410 million cubic metres (11.61 m³) of water, weighing about 400 million tons. The resulting currents and tidal races gain additional strength and complexity thanks to the funnel shape of the Channel. It is not surprising that the Bristol Channel is a challenge for sailors. Patricia Cairns, a teacher of mathematics at the College, found the Bristol Channel as tough and as challenging as any of the conditions she had faced on the world's oceans.[6]

Desmond Hoare, thanks to his naval training, was quite clear about the risks – and the opportunities. He was later to write:

> *Our sailing is conducted in the most dangerous waters in which I have operated small boats. Before we opened the school, all the local experts said we would never sail dinghies off our beach. The Deputy Chief Inspector, RNLI, has said that we probably have the most difficult operating conditions of any of their fifty or so other Inshore Rescue Boat stations around the coast of Britain … we have a tidal race a mile to the East and another a mile to the West … the spring tides run at five knots off our foreshore …*

But he and Hahn had found what they were looking for, a place in which to bring to life the message of the first prospectus:

5   These figures are taken from Desmond Hoare's training notes for the College lifeboat crews.
6   Patricia Cairns crewed for Dr David Lewis and his family on a world voyage in the course of which David Lewis retraced the approximate route of eastern Polynesian migration to New Zealand, using only the traditional Polynesian methods of navigation. Patricia acted as his navigational safety officer, her instruments and calculations entirely withheld from him to ensure the validity of his investigations.

Boys must be encouraged to achieve physical fitness and to learn the necessary techniques which will permit them to work for others and to do this in situations which can also satisfy their instinct for adventure. To this end we have planned our rescue services: beach rescue, canoe life guards, and cliff rescue. Nothing convinces as much as does the saving of life that the common humanity of men is more important than race or colour. The recognition of this by youth … must, we feel, make some contribution to peace.

St Donatus is the holy patron and protector of seamen. The old Welsh name for St Donat's had been *Abergwaredwyr* – 'the meeting place of rescuing men.'

This prize-winning photograph was to become the college's 'trademark' in the national press.

Sir Edward Stradling (1529–1609), mentioned earlier, was a notable scholar who commissioned an important grammar of the Welsh language and provided for the endowment of the very distinguished grammar school in Cowbridge. He bequeathed to his successors his personal motto: '*Vertue's whole praise consisteth in doing.*'

The Atlantic College was to take all of this to heart.

CHAPTER 2
The College's Early Years

Desmond Hoare became a retired Rear-Admiral on 1st January 1962 and by September 1962 had assembled teaching staff and students. The Castle was ready to receive its new occupants for living, eating, sleeping, study and recreation, and only the science laboratories and most of the staff accommodation were 'extra-mural'. It was the first major international boarding school to open in Britain and the first sixth-form college. There were 56 students from 15 countries, the staff British except for a German instructor in seamanship who had been a former officer on the sail training ship *Pamir*, and an Australian.

The pattern of life was rapidly established. All students took three A-Level courses together with two or three subsidiary-level subjects – the non-British students to ensure they met the university entry requirements of their home countries, the British because the narrow approach to sixth-form education was resisted as a matter of principle. Alec Peterson of the Oxford Department of Education, a fervent advocate of a broader curriculum, was an influential member of the Founding Committee. Worries that students working in a foreign language would be handicapped in qualifying for their university entry were set at rest by the first examination results in 1964, which were convincingly above the British national average. In support was a wide programme of activities – physical (but the term 'sport' was not used), cultural, and the rescue services.

The build-up in numbers was steady. By 1964 the demand already exceeded the number of places – 156 students were enrolled from 21 countries, 90 of them on scholarships. By the fifth academic year there were 235 students from 35 countries, including Czechoslovakia and Poland, the first from the Socialist bloc.

This hole through the massive concrete sea wall was created in 1962 to enable College sea-going.

The scholarship element was of capital importance. Entry was to be independent not only of race, religion and politics but also of financial background. Writing in *The Spectator* in June 1965, Alec Peterson reported that, of the 68 British boys in the college, 55 were from local authority schools on local or trade union scholarships and, of the other 21 nations represented, 12 had scholarship schemes and 6 more were considering them.

All of this required intensive public relations, fundraising and negotiations overseas.

Kurt Hahn had received a very encouraging letter as early as June 1961 from the office of the Federal Chancellor Konrad Adenauer in Bonn, and in 1963 the College received its first governmental support – £45,000 from Germany, followed by a second grant in 1965 of £27,000, a total of £72,000. Stirred no doubt by this precedent, the British government followed suit in 1964 with £50,000, with two supplementary grants raising the total to £100,000. A remarkable feature of these grants was that they were approved successively by Conservative and Labour administrations.

British business, banks and foundations, with the Dulverton Trust and the Bernard Sunley Charitable Foundation in the lead, added their support to that of many generous individuals. An especially significant endorsement came from the Ford Foundation which, in 1963, made a grant of $140,000, the first time in its history that it had given money to education below university level in Great Britain or Europe.

In heavy weather the waves surge up past the lifeboat station and workshops.

American educators were now taking a serious interest, and later visitors included the Director of the Stanford University International Development and Education Centre, the Chairman of the National Committee on the Assessment of Education, and the Dean of Harvard.

Here, it is important to state that the College would have gone under in 1964 had Sir George Schuster not put his shoulder to the wheel. Sir George had enjoyed a career of astonishing variety and influence in banking, colonial administration at the highest levels, Parliament and local government, and characteristically valued among his most valuable experiences that of his close cooperation with the Labour Minister Aneurin Bevan in the introduction of the British National Health Service. It had also fallen to him to save Voluntary Service Overseas (VSO) from financial collapse and disaster. Frustrated by what he perceived as the very inefficient conduct of Atlantic College business in 1964, he agreed to chair an emergency committee at a time when there were enough funds in the bank for one more month of operation only. His sole condition was that it be called 'The

Desmond Hoare, Lawrance Darvall and George and Gwen Schuster as the foundation stone is laid for the new science laboratories.

Action Committee'. He was 83 and had been looking for a challenge to keep him happily occupied in his old age!

In 1964 the Duke of Edinburgh spent several hours at the College. The following year both he and the Queen were at St Donat's, the College having to secure special authorisation from the London University Examinations Board to alter the timing of certain A-Level papers to allow the students to show their paces.

Academic barriers and solutions

The first prospectus had referred to the huge problems, unimaginable today, faced by parents working abroad who wished to keep their families together, sending their children to a local school yet wanting to be able to enrol them in universities back at home. Neither the curricula nor the examinations existed to make this possible:

> *It is inconceivable that such barriers will exist at the turn of the century. Nevertheless, we have yet to remove them ... the force of example is needed and, to be effective in this area of strongly entrenched views and practices, it must be on a scale and of an academic stature to carry conviction. The Atlantic College project is aimed at setting this example.*

A main task of the College was therefore the setting up of bi-lateral agreements over the equivalence of school-leaving certificates as qualifications for university entry. These were intended as a useful interim step on the way towards a truly international examination and were successfully achieved for all students entering the College. From the start, it was normal for all leavers to go on to university unless they had national military service obligations which took precedence.

The College was naturally anxious to play an active role in the creation and acceptance of a widely accepted International Baccalaureate (IB) and soon joined forces with colleagues in the International School in Geneva and the United Nations School in New York in pursuit of this aim. In 1967 the first IB examinations were tested in some 20 countries in nine subjects. From 1968 Atlantic College students found themselves sitting these examinations, the American College Board Scholastic Aptitude and Achievement Tests and their critical A-Levels as part of a research programme to measure comparability between the different systems. The A-Level programme was abandoned from the 1971 entry. Henceforward all students were entered for the ground-breaking IB Diploma. As was widely foreseen by IB adherents, they rapidly became more attractive candidates for university admissions tutors than their standard A-Level fellows.

Other important developments

All this progress gave encouragement to those who wanted to press ahead with similar colleges in other countries. Already by 1963, the enthusiastic endorsement of some major personalities in public life in North America had been secured, including Senator J. William Fulbright and Ambassador Adlai Stevenson and, most significantly, the Canadian Prime Minister Lester Pearson. Lester Pearson was later to visit St Donat's twice. After his death in 1972 his many friends, with the generous support of the Canadian government, were to set up Pearson College on Vancouver Island in his memory.

The first girls to arrive (1967) generate some predictable interest and attention.

Critics had meanwhile not hesitated to question one dimension of the project. Why was it, a puzzled journalist asked in 1965, that you are ready to educate only one half of the human race? Desmond Hoare, who had two daughters and one son, never had doubts on the matter. He told the journalist that, if someone would give him £40,000, he would commission a girls' house the following day. The comment duly appeared in the next issue of the *Sunday Express*; an Italo-American couple, delayed at Geneva Airport, thumbed through the newspapers; and a bank in

Before long they had become fully integrated – here seen refuelling a lifeboat after a night exercise afloat.

London telephoned the College a few days later to ask what they should do with a cheque that had just arrived for £40,000. Sonny and Phebe Maresi had embarked on one of the great friendships of their lives with George Schuster and were soon the biggest individual donors to the Atlantic College. The Governing Body was taken aback, there was some dissension in the ranks, one or two resigned, and the initial donation went not to a girls' dormitory but to completion of the science building. Nonetheless the first girls entered the College in 1967 as regular students rather than, as had already happened, privately as the daughters of the Headmaster and of the Bursar. With all these achievements and the arrival of a period of rather greater financial stability, the scene was set for Desmond Hoare, at his own suggestion and urging, to step down from the headship in 1969 and devote himself to expansion of the entire project overseas.

In retrospect it all sounds so easy and inevitable, and a student writing his thesis for the Canberra College of Advanced Education summarised it a little airily as '*a triumph of inspiration and zealous and dedicated activity on the part of a number of loosely coordinated upper-echelon idealists who had connections in the right places at the right levels and on whom fortune had smiled at the right moments*'. No account given later can give adequate expression to the stress and strain, numbing anxieties and sheer hard slog of the early days for those in the senior positions of responsibility, and the protagonists would probably not have recalled their efforts in those words. But the story of the United World Colleges moves in distinct chapters, and by 1969 the first chapter had been written.

And now to those boats![7]

7   Those boats, having started out as 'Inflatables', became 'Inshore Rescue Boats' (IRBs) in the early years of the College. They mutated, seemingly without any conscious decision but presumably in order to contrast them with 'Offshore Lifeboats', into 'Inshore Lifeboats' (ILBs). Once the type became widely used outside the rescue world, they became Rigid Inflatable Boats (RIBs). In this account I use the term 'Inshore Lifeboats' for their time at Atlantic College and, alas, 'Rigid Inflatable Boats' thereafter. The term used by the Dutch Life Saving Society seems to me the most appropriate: 'Rigid Hull Inflatables'.

CHAPTER 3
Excitement and Challenge

Desmond Hoare at the time the College opened.

'It is', wrote Desmond Hoare, '*one of the firmest of College rules that students are to stay alive.*' Good advice for those going out on the Bristol Channel most days of the year, especially in the winter months! An important rule too, for there was nothing to the west between the College and the USA save sea and turbulent tides. Maritime activities against a background of severe natural hazards were however nothing new for the Channel.

The first students arrived almost simultaneously with the first boats: two small inflatables, six small single-handed Minisails and six Fireball dinghies, new on the market. Desmond Hoare had immediately recognised the qualities of the Fireball at the Earls Court Boat Show the previous January – exciting to handle, quick on to the plane and therefore quick to drain, easy to right from a capsize and highly suitable for challenging conditions of tide, current and waves. The College bought 6 of the first 36 to be made. But the first winter left the students in no doubt about the challenges ahead. The Randolph Hearst sea-water swimming pool froze over, and all 56 students had themselves photographed standing together on the ice. Ice even formed on the rocky edges of the Bristol Channel itself.

The May 1963 issue of the College magazine brings all these things back to mind. Here are the curiously eloquent words of the College sailing instructor, Captain Rainer von Barsewisch, first mate in 1957 on the last commercial voyage of a four-mast barque, the German sail training vessel **Passat**:

Our Sailing Club had been in a pretty bad state in its development so far. There was the worm in it ... everything played against us, the weather in particular ... in the only two races we had dared to attempt, we had been blown to pieces in the one, and covered and suffocated by fog in the other ... and we had a hard winter behind us ... digging our boats out of the snow and dragging them over lumps of ice whenever necessary, but nevertheless it had sorted out the good and the better boy.

But, on a windy and rough day in Barry, they found their compensations:

The sea was so steep over the bar and off the harbour entrance, that the dinghies jumped like dolphins, digging their bows deep into the coming waves, being thrown up by rolling crests and almost flung into the air while the new trough deepened under them ... it was wonderful to see how [she] broke free again, water pouring out of the cockpit, as she lifted herself, accelerating, on to the new plane ... the most exciting sight is probably when they run before wind and tide, picking up the most unbelievable speed as they slide down the front of the waves, leaving a solid wall of spray on either side ... the old Barry Club boatswain who helmed our safety launch was absolutely

The Fireball, a magnificent sailing craft and a fine boat in which to teach adventurous beginners.

The first winter, 1962–3, was a hard one. No swimming!

thrilled … I don't think I shall ever forget the moment when he held out his handker-chief, like a toreador. One Fireball raced up to us, covered in spray, all three members hanging out over the side, one on the trapeze, and as the boat roared past we saw a hand reaching out, grabbing the handkerchief, and suddenly the three faces, simply burning with vigour and excitement …

An excited article in *The Western Mail* abandoned all journalistic criteria for objective reporting:

Even in Barry Harbour the boat was very soon half-full from her own bow wave. However, it must be remembered that the college's requirements are not the same as those of an ordinary yacht club … the idea is to make the boys tough, and the Fireball would certainly help with that. With this boat the crew only come up for air about once every five minutes, and a schnorkel with an air tube to the masthead will be almost as essential as a trapeze …

But how was all this possible?

It all came down to rubber – rubber suits and rubber boats – and some inspired empirical innovation.

The Rubber Suits and the Discipline of the Situation

Desmond Hoare had already bemused naval apprentices in Plymouth by appearing on the beach wearing a rubber suit with 'TARZAN' in large yellow letters across his chest. The estate staff at St Donat's was not less astonished to observe

First make your skin suit! An instructional panel on the wall illustrates the patterns that were developed by Naomi Hoare.

their new Headmaster, some months before the College opened, floating on his back in the Bristol Channel, smoking his pipe and, as he explained, testing the strength of the local currents. But it was Naomi Hoare who now became the key figure.

Naomi was able to draw on enviable family talent and distinction. Her forebears had dominated British architecture for the past century. Her father, Adrian Gilbert Scott, was the grandson of Sir George Gilbert Scott, the son of George Gilbert Scott, the nephew of John Oldrid Scott and the brother of Sir Giles Gilbert Scott. Among the family's achievements have been: The Martyrs' Memorial in St Giles, Oxford; London's St Pancras Station; the Albert Memorial in London's Hyde Park; the Foreign and Commonwealth Office in Whitehall; Liverpool Anglican Cathedral; the Battersea Power Station on the South Bank of the River Thames and the Bankside Power Station which has recently been converted into the Tate Modern Art Gallery; the Cambridge University Library; the design and rebuilding of the House of Commons after its war-time destruction in 1941 and the classical, at one time ubiquitous, red telephone kiosk. Fiercely reluctant to leave her fine Hampstead home for 'this mad venture in Wales', Naomi nonetheless rapidly immersed herself and her quite formidable energies in the new challenges. An untiring hostess of students and of the innumerable visitors, all of whom required VIP attention, she also became a truly remarkable helm of the Fireball dinghy and a highly competent instructor, able to hold her own in the toughest weather. Now she applied her dressmaking skills to the elusive and devious qualities of neoprene rubber. After some experimentation, she developed a series of patterns that enabled her to measure every single student and member of staff who opted for sea-going activities over the coming seven years (the average number each year was around 100). Each of them received a sheet of neoprene with their personal templates drawn on it. It remained only for them to cut them out with care and glue them together in the prescribed order.

This was a rapid introduction both to team work and to the English language. Very soon after their arrival, these students from 30 and more different countries found themselves engaged on a shared, unusual and wholly unexpected task that absorbed their interest completely, tested their manual skills, generated spontaneous and friendly competition, and proved to be a highly effective avenue for creating lasting friendships. For many, the early students in particular, the gluing sessions which took place in the library, the classrooms and the dormitories created memories that are inseparable from the smell of glue and, before the days of neoprene with nylon lining, talcum powder with which to ease the suits on and off. For one student, 'the fact that one made one's own skin suit was beyond belief ...', for another, 'the smell of neoprene, the sense of impending adventure'.

... but first you had to get afloat.

The cold waters of the Bristol Channel were a strong incentive for good workmanship and a close fit.

For Naomi Hoare it could have brought wider fame as she was invited to the Ritz Hotel in London by the makers of James Bond film *Thunderball* to measure up Sean Connery for a skin suit, but her hospitality commitments at the College took precedence.

Desmond Hoare's foremost educational principle was to insist on the '*discipline of the situation*'. The Bristol Channel was the chosen 'situation', and the constant seeping of freezing Channel water through badly glued joints was a first-rate incentive for good rubber-suit workmanship. College students wandering round the quiet and rural village of Llandyssul in mid-Wales in October 1962, with their rubber tails swinging between their legs whilst engaged in a project week of canoeing, generated some real fear among the locals that the world had been invaded, but the fact of the matter was that the successful completion of one's neoprene skin suit was a fine educational experience and achievement. Their use was the first key to all the subsequent marine accomplishments of the College and the reason why the students were able to make such an impression on the highly experienced and tough sailors of the Yacht Club in Barry.

Not only was the College the first organisation, ahead even of the military, to adopt the neoprene suit as standard equipment; it was also the College, in the person of Naomi Hoare, working hard over a Christmas vacation, that made the world's first one-piece suits, which were more economical, quicker to make, and infinitely more suitable for their purpose. It took some time nonetheless for the word to get around, at least in Britain. An author writing about the RNLI in 1967 was to praise the Scuba wet suit which, he had discovered, was now being used experimentally by the US Coastguard: '*Tests*', he reported '*have shown that the Scuba wet suits keep life-boatmen warm and dry during long periods of rescue work*

... is there an idea here for the [RNLI] Institution?' By that time well over 500 students had successfully braved UK winter weather at sea in all conditions without any ill effect whatever on their health. And the British marine scene had been enriched by a new word, 'frost-biting', coined by the College's students from Norway pushing the boundaries in their second language.

The Rubber Boats

The second application of rubber was the inflatable boat, made famous in recent times by the Frenchman Dr Barnard when he drifted across the Atlantic in a 15-foot inflatable raft in 1952, taking 65 days and assisted only by a small lug sail. Inflated animal skins have been used for centuries to assist people and goods across water – a stone plaque in the British Museum shows figures swimming across a river 2,500 years ago supported by inflated animal skins. The Duke of Wellington is said to have experimented with inflatable craft carrying troops and supplies across the Thames. But the most intriguing account of early inflatables is given in *Pleasure Boating in the Victorian Era* by P. A. L. Vine, published in 1983. In 1843 a young lieutenant in the Royal Navy, Peter Halkett, constructed a boat-cloak or cloak-boat, so-called because it could be worn as a cloak until needed as a boat. Quickly inflated by bellows, its total weight including bellows and paddles was about 5 kg (12 lb). Halkett made experimental voyages, among other places on the English south coast, in the Bay of Dublin and even the Bay of Biscay, where he was authorised to demonstrate his invention before a fleet of naval men-of-war, propelling it in turn by paddle and by the use of his umbrella-sail. The Admiralty commissioned several to be made in the belief that they might be suitable as ship's lifeboats. The famous explorer Sir John Franklin was to state that, had he had one on his first journey to the Polar Sea in 1819–21, he might have foregone much distress and saved the lives of those who died of famine and fatigue when he was unable to cross the Copper Mine River. He took one with him on his last and ill-fated journey in 1845.

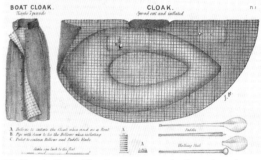

Halkett's Boat Cloak, constructed of macintosh India-rubber cloth with paddle, umbrella sail and bellows.

John MacGregor, the noted author on canoeing, records in his diary on 22nd May 1848 that he had met Archibald Smith (of Trinity College, Cambridge, and a Fellow of the Royal Society), with his *'india-rubber boat which forms a cloak, tent, boat and bed'*. Rubber boats began to be manufactured commercially by a firm in Charing Cross, London, and it is also reported that at least one of their boats was made for the expedition to search for Dr Livingstone. In 1862 Halkett was awarded

The Boat Cloak under sail, 1844.

Inflatables Large and Small

Amphitrite, constructed in 1960 as a joint venture of Jacques Cousteau's Calypso Group and the *National Geographic Magazine*, was at the time the world's largest inflatable vessel (65 by 27 ft). The U-shaped hull was made of rip-resistant nylon-neoprene fabric supplied by the French company Zodiac with nine sealed compartments. When fully laden with expeditionary gear, five men and a 2,000 mile fuel supply, the fast-skimming craft drew only fourteen inches of water. She was planned as a prototype for vessels that might be deflated, taken apart and boxed up for airlift to remote places, there to be reassembled, pumped up and launched from beaches on pneumatic rollers. Engine power was to be supplied by diesel and water jet, although the urgency of completing her for her ceremonial launch in Nice led to the initial fitting of eight 80 horsepower outboards. She carried a diving saucer, the Denise, the first underwater vehicle designed expressly for scientific exploration, able to work 350 metres below the surface for up to five hours. A

standard orthodox vessel would have weighed 55 tons. *Amphitrite* fully loaded weighed in at 5 tons. She is shown here on her three-mile journey through the streets of Nice for her ceremonial launch on 10th December 1960.

Antonin Besse, the donor of St Donat's Castle, was a friend, sponsor and diving colleague of Jacques Cousteau, having first met him when he was experimenting with car inner tubes for making masks for use under water. He accompanied him on several voyages of underwater exploration to the Farsan Islands, the Seychelles and the Amirantes, sharing a cabin on the trip to the Seychelles with the film maker Louis Malle, who subsequently produced Cousteau's *The Silent World*. Before leaving for the Seychelles they called on the Sultan of Abu Dhabi, Sheikh Shakhbout. The annual income of Abu Dhabi was then £7,500. Later, Cousteau's mother ship, *Calypso*, had extensive repairs undertaken free of charge in the Aden Dockyard, a shipyard of the Besse Group.

LEFT: Contemporary advertisement for the Boat Cloak.

RIGHT: Contemporary advertisement for the Knapsack-Boat, which won Lieutenant Halkett a prize medal in the International Exhibition of 1862.

a prize medal by the Commissioners of the International Exhibition for his 8-foot-long rubber knapsack boat which could carry two people. It was not however until the Second World War that inflatable boats were manufactured in their thousands as emergency rescue craft for air forces. Yet more time went by before their peace-time potential was recognised and exploited. '*A long labour – a difficult birth – and a bouncing baby*' is the expressive title of a manuscript account which lies in the RNLI archives in Poole. It was written by David Stogdon, a major figure in our story.

David Stogdon was first shown an inflatable by the RFD Company in the 1950s. They claimed it would make a satisfactory rescue craft. After looking at it, David Stogdon was convinced that his RNLI colleagues would have none of it, nor would they ever entrust the lives of their lifeboat crews to untrustworthy out-board engines. But he was then impressed by the decision of the Head of the Fire Service in Jersey to use an inflatable and trailer for the rescue of casualties around the island coast – and tourist lives were especially valuable![8] In fact, the message was on the wall for those with eyes to see – the growth in leisure marine activities was leading to a sharply accelerating requirement for inshore as opposed to off-shore rescue. Captain Edmonton in Jersey was happily able to count on admirable assistance, given informally by the island RNLI station, but the legal situation remained that the RNLI covered lifesaving from shipwreck; beach and inshore casualties were the responsibility of local councils. Nor did the RNLI, dependent then as now entirely on voluntary contributions, have the funds to spend on inno-vative and costly development outside their recognised areas of activity!

But then two private citizens, Norman Cavell, the Honorary Secretary of the Walmer Lifeboat, and Alfred Schermuly, the owner of the Schermuly Rocket Company and manufacturer of emergency marine flares, took over personal and financial responsibility for bringing the experimentation to the stage where it could safely and confidently be brought to the attention of the RNLI Committee of Management. Even so, it required the enlightened support of the former First Officer of the **Queen Mary**, Captain Tony Wicksteed, now RNLI Deputy Chief Inspector. Sceptics may like to apply the caution one normally attributes to anglers' tales, but this is David Stogdon's account. On the one day that Wicksteed could spare for a personal assessment it was blowing a Force 7 gale. The small RFD inflatable with four aboard made a winter evening tour of a Polish fishing fleet that was sheltering at anchor off Walmer on the south-east coast. Wicksteed, adequately impressed, authorised further official trials.

Stogdon expressed much admiration and gratitude towards the French who, in Brittany in the early 1960s, were already well advanced in the use of the inflatable

8 This Jersey initiative has an interesting match with the decision taken in 1952 by Reg Blanchford, the Head of the Guernsey St John Ambulance, to purchase and equip a former RAF high-speed rescue launch as a marine ambulance, a decision he took entirely on his own and to the anger of some local doctors, but which proved highly successful.

for inshore rescue. One of their most important insights was to ensure that their crews were trained to be 'part of the water', and a crew member was always put over the side, on a line, to assist the casualty in the water before the boat came alongside. Small wheels were fixed to the transom, enabling easy boat launch from exposed beaches.

Interestingly, in the light of the later Atlantic College and Kurt Hahn connection, Stogdon goes on to state that *'probably the most valuable support came from Aberdovey Outward Bound Sea School'*. Aberdovey was the first of Kurt Hahn's Outward Bound schools, founded in 1941 with the generous support of one of his Gordonstoun parents, Lawrence Holt, the Chairman of the Liverpool Blue Funnel line. Captain Freddy Fuller, the first Warden, a really significant figure in the early days of Outward Bound – a protagonist of the 'drown-proofing' survival technique, and a consultant at the launch of President Kennedy's Peace Corps – took the trial inflatable out over the Aberdovey Bar in strong gale-force winds from the west. *'Without any fuss, Captain Fuller took the rubber boat out by himself and disappeared from view. I asked the senior instructor whether he would launch the old 35 foot Liverpool lifeboat if Captain Fuller needed assistance. He replied that the weather was too severe to launch.'* As happens in all the best stories, Captain Fuller reappeared none the worse, said he had never been in any kind of danger, and *'his only difficulty was in knowing in which direction he was travelling as he could see nothing on the bar'*.

Developing technology was now achieving huge improvements in the toughness and weather resistance of flexible fabrics, and the inflatable and foldable rubber boat soon became almost a standard feature as a beach toy, tender for yachts and lightweight craft for military operations.

The merits of the inflatable for rescue purposes spring immediately to mind: buoyancy in all conditions, much enhanced by the possibility of having multiple independent cells of air; ease of going alongside a stricken craft without the banging together of hard topsides; and the related ease of hauling a helpless casualty aboard without inflicting additional injury, especially in rough waters. A 9 foot dinghy having a 4 foot 4 inch beam has a volume of enclosed buoyancy of approximately 1,200 lb and will have a total displacement approaching a ton. Such a boat, even if flooded with water, will still support as many people as can physically be packed into it. The wide beam and flat base give excellent stability, being far more stable than a rigid craft of similar dimensions. The resilient structure gives the craft the ability to bounce off solid objects such as rocks without damage.

The immediate weaknesses are perhaps equally obvious: the constraint on the power of engine that can be attached safely to the stern; the consequent limit in speed over the water, especially rough water; and the tendency of the inflatable to fold – any body without a skeleton will flex and give way – with the resulting limitation in size and carrying capacity. These weaknesses had to be put into the context of new needs around the British coast.

This was the point at which the Atlantic College came on the scene.

Dramatic offshore operations — made unforgettable on 27th April 1947 in Wales when all members of The Mumbles Lifeboat were lost in their desperate, courageous attempt to rescue the crew of the stricken *Samtampa* off Sker Point, and in 1953 in Scotland with the deaths of twelve crew of the Fraserburgh and Arbroath lifeboats, one survivor only from each boat — had hitherto defined the RNLI image in the public mind. Now, there emerged the growing need to respond rapidly to inshore incidents — amateur yachtsmen and small boat owners who, with the explosion in the number of pleasure craft, were joining holiday-makers, coastal walkers and surfboard riders in increasing numbers in requiring assistance and rescue. A newspaper article reporting the elderly couple who had driven their new motor boat from Falmouth to Minehead in the Bristol Channel, equipped only with a road map, was an eloquent example. It was becoming urgently necessary to be able to reach shallow-water areas that were inaccessible to the traditional lifeboat, with rapid response times and speed over the water. A fast rescue capability close to the shore also implied the necessity of being able to launch from the beach. By 1971, the Royal Yachting Association was to note in the winter issue of its journal that year that

increased leisure, together with the increased affluence of the population, has caused something of an explosion, to the point where services to pleasure vessels are now running at double the number of those to fishing vessels and, because of improvement in navigational aids, the RNLI have to do less work on the preservation of life from commercial shipwreck ...

and

... a 70 per cent increase in the number of services to unidentified distress signals ... coastguard are thinner on the ground and therefore more often responding to hearsay reports rather than actual observation.

The trend was unstoppable. In a July 2008 publication the RNLI was to record that in the previous year, 2007, 52% of launches were to leisure craft users, 28% to people not using any kind of craft, 12% to merchant or fishing vessels and 8% to other sea users.

Thanks above all to the work of David Stogdon and Tony Wicksteed, the RNLI began its response. The folding fabric inflatable was, within certain constraints, a very safe boat. A new chapter was opening. It coincided with and owed much to a sharp decline in the numbers of professional coastal seamen and a simultaneous growth of expertise in experimental boat design and technological capabilities. The new challenges found new solutions.

CHAPTER 4
The College – its Needs and its Opportunity

Shortly before the Atlantic College opened in 1962, a friend offered Desmond Hoare a personal gift of £500 to spend on anything he liked for the school. He chose a 13 foot 6 inch RFD folding inflatable (so called after the company's founder, Reginald Foster Dagnall) with a 20 hp Evinrude outboard engine, the whole capable of just over 17 knots, and the Easter holiday of 1962 saw the experimental launch of a boat from the St Donat's foreshore for the first time in living memory.

The College proposed to run marine activities, including dinghy sailing, off the St Donat's foreshore five or six afternoons a week throughout the year. It had to achieve safety, but it also offered a remarkable practical laboratory for experimentation in equipment and training.

By the time the College opened, inflatables were already being fitted with wooden floor boards inserted over the fabric floors. The French company producing the well-known Zodiac boats had also designed and fitted an ingenious inflatable keel tube which gave much improved directional stability at relatively high speeds. But these folding floors were no match for the Bristol Channel and collapsed easily, especially when the pressure in the tubes was low. Low pressure in the tubes was frequently caused by the cooling effect of bringing a boat from warmer conditions onshore into the cold waters of the Channel.

Even more serious was the failure of the fabric floors through abrasion, hardly a surprise to those stumbling over the rocky channel foreshore off St Donat's, carrying the boats to the water's edge, then fitting the engines before launching; and one commented later, '*I remember the numerous times we had to crawl back against the tide, sitting on the tubes and holding the petrol tank and the bottom of the boat up because everything had come loose.*' Later experience suggested that the life of the inflatable tube, housed in the open and driven at sea for an average of two hours a day from January to December, was three years, and the equivalent in distance to travelling more than once round the world, but the floors were being damaged beyond easy repair within days, especially at the transom end. It was proving next to impossible to keep two boats serviceable out of the three available, and one rescue boat alone at sea for up to 12 sailing craft was clearly unsafe. The RNLI was of course facing the same problem. It attempted to solve it by half-measures – cutting out the rear section of floor fabric and replacing it with a piece of ply to match the shape of the fabric floor it was replacing. The predictable result was to move the wear problem forward to the join between the plywood floor and the floor fabric.

As the original idea behind the inflatable boats was ease of transport onshore, the wooden floors were made in sections to allow disassembly in small components. The first step was to replace the internal sectional and folding floor with a single sheet of ply, an immediate improvement, but then the question arose: why keep the fabric floor under the boat where it is so susceptible to damage? The answer: it doesn't work, throw it out. Attach the wooden floor directly to the tube and do away completely with the fabric!

BELOW LEFT: *The tubes were expensive and in short supply in the early days and, as can be seen here, carried the evidence of being used time and time again.*

BELOW RIGHT: *An early example of the line and reel for a swimmer. Work on these early boats often required considerable flexibility of limb!*

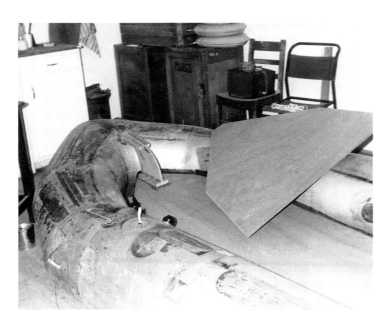

This key modification was possible because the College boats were not deflated and folded up after each sea-going session. Lessons learned from making skin suits were valuable but not enough, for it was now a question of attaching rubber to wood. All the mating surfaces in both materials had to be roughened up, and the chosen instrument was the broken hacksaw blade. But it worked. The first experimental craft was completed and even won a prize in a local powerboat race on a rough day when other small speed boats were breaking up or flooding.

This early success in attaching tube and floor to one another solved urgent maintenance problems but led to serious instability at sea. How many would be ready to fix a powerful engine to the back of an upturned dining-room table and drive it at speed in a seaway? The next solution was adopted from the increasingly popular surfboards with the fitting of simple vertical fins under the hull, but these in turn made the boats impossible to land and to transport on trolleys.

One account from the early days gives an Argentinean student the credit for having sparked some new thinking. Chatting with Bob Hale, the boat workshop and swimming-pool attendant at the time, this student had wondered about raising the floor and letting the boat ride only on its tubes for greater speed. His reward for this thinking was the task, with a small group of fellow students, of scraping yet more rubber and remodelling the smallest boat which happened to be awaiting repair. In smooth water the result turned out to be faster than the other inflatables but lacked any directional stability and, with its cushion of air underneath, was unsafe in going upwind. The next stage was to create a hull that roughly followed the lines of the tube. This was more successful; she '*cut cleanly through the waves, turned on a point, landed squarely when she became airborne, and sped past all the other boats*'. During the summer holiday, the two principal builders took her out to the Mediterranean, the boat travelling separately. '*Getting*

An early boat. She carries a large timber locker over the bow for equipment and features two seats aft glued to the tube for helmsman and crew.

ABOVE LEFT: *A very early attempt, with fins, to give the tube some directional stability at sea. These fins did not long survive landings on trolleys or rocky beaches! It can also be seen here that the plywood hull, raised well within the rubber tube, was unable to make any contribution at all to the sea-keeping qualities of the boat.*

ABOVE RIGHT: *Another modest attempt at giving the hull directional stability with fins. Here the hard hull is at least in direct contact with the water. Note also that the transom is fixed for the first time directly to the wooden hull, thereby ensuring that the engine power is transmitted directly to the hard hull.*

LEFT: *This compromise ensured the safe use of trolleys.*

the thing from the rail station to the canal was hard work, and getting it out to sea past hundreds of gigantic freighters from all over the world was harrowing. Once we were on our way, however, it was great fun. We encountered German nudists, fire ants, food poisoning, and total indifference from the French life guards whose Zodiacs appeared never to have been launched.' The final problem was persuading a British customs officer to allow an American student to re-enter the UK with an outboard engine in his personal luggage.

It was at this stage in the College's marine affairs, on 28th October 1963, that, in Desmond Hoare's words, *'we received with respectful astonishment a visit by the*

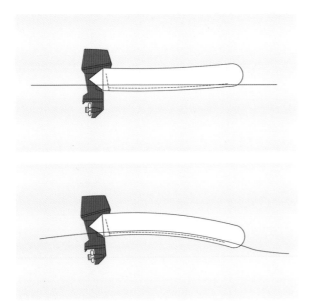

ABOVE LEFT: *Engine power once applied alters the shape of a fully flexible tube and glues it to the water surface.*

ABOVE RIGHT: *Naomi Hoare is enrolled to produce better seats for the early boats.*

top brass of the RNLI who, to our further amazement, requested our advice. So began a continuing happy relationship. Nevertheless, at this very point our ways began to diverge.' This visit led to the provision of a series of inflatables by the RNLI which the College was requested to drive as hard as possible, and indeed four such boats had been driven to a write-off state by 1967. However, the College needs indeed differed from those of the RNLI.

When on the plane, the fabric floor of the inflatable towards the stern is pushed upwards by the force of the water. This produces a curved shape longitudinally which acts like an aerofoil, giving lift downwards and thus gluing the boat to the surface. The more the power, the stronger the 'glue'! However, the maximum speed attainable on such craft is in the region of 20 knots and the use of more than 40 hp distorts the boat and eventually breaks the transom away from the tubes.

With the surf running in to the College beach most days of the year at about 16 knots, a maximum speed of 20 knots was unacceptable as it made it impossible to manoeuvre between one breaker and the next. It was this basic safety need that forced the next logical stage in development – the bringing together of the qualities of the inflatable with the speed and seaworthiness of the finest craft of the powerboat racing world.

Early Problems and Early Solutions

Whilst the problems rapidly became clear, the early solutions had been rudimentary. However, the critical first step had been achieved – the bonding of a rigid floor directly with the tube. This would lead by 1964 to the concept of a hollow rigid floor which would provide a hydrodynamic underwater shape for fast sea-going in rough water, longitudinal strength with no flexing, the ability to manage greater engine power, and greatly reduced maintenance problems – all of these wedded with the widely recognised merits of the soft inflatable tube for coming alongside and for handling casualties. The rigid-hulled inflatable had been born. Other very important advantages were to become quickly apparent, including the immediate fitting of foot straps that were clearly essential for crew safety, but there remained a vital and immediate constraint: the hulls had to be designed to fit existing, commercially produced tubes.

The boats constructed in the first two years by College students had romantic names – *Freya*, *Bacchus*, *Atalanta*, *Triton*, *Aphrodite*. All were eventually sea-worthy and all managed some 20 knots with crews of two or three. *Bacchus*, the first, once lost her engine when the stern tore apart. The engine

was found at low tide and restored to use. Safety retainer chains from engine to transom prevented further such losses. But *Bacchus* was sufficiently successful to encourage two more hulls along the same general lines. She was deeper in the forefront than aft, in imitation of the Zodiac design. Later designs took a straight and deep V from bow to stern. This improved their seaworthiness but made them difficult to handle on trolleys, an essential piece of equipment in beach launch and recovery. The time had come, however, to forego romance. The College developments were beginning to attract serious attention. The future craft were all given X names – X for experimental – from 1964 onwards.

The building of X1 began in June 1964. Her overall length, with the tube overhanging both the bow of the rigid hull and aft of the transom, was 16 feet, the

The hard hull of the rigid inflatable begins to take shape. It can be seen clearly here, however, how the hull shape is dictated by the flat lines of the pre-existing tube.

This type of trolly required the boats to be lifted off and re-positioned between every seagoing session.

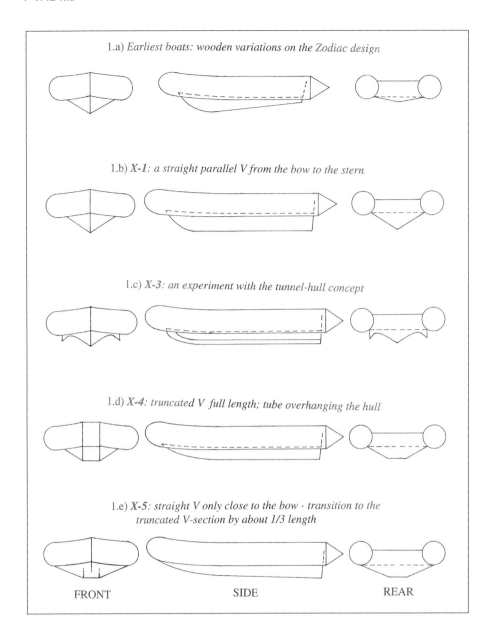

1.a) *Earliest boats: wooden variations on the Zodiac design*

1.b) *X-1: a straight parallel V from the bow to the stern*

1.c) *X-3: an experiment with the tunnel-hull concept*

1.d) *X-4: truncated V full length; tube overhanging the hull*

1.e) *X-5: straight V only close to the bow - transition to the truncated V-section by about 1/3 length*

FRONT   SIDE   REAR

wooden hull 13 feet. Her floor was V-sectioned with a roughly 20-degree constant deadrise, with 9 inches of depth on a 4-foot wide floor, the floor being installed with the upper surface 1 inch above the bottom of the Dunlop Gemini air tubes. The floor was strengthened internally at the stern and, another innovation, the wooden transom was secured to the floor with oak knees rather than relying solely on bonding with the tube. In this manner the thrust of the 40 hp outboard engine was transmitted directly to the wooden floor and the water friction was overcome more efficiently. The wooden hull now became the major shock absorber, with the tube in a supporting role, 'ridden' by the crew for greater comfort. It soon became clear, however, that there was serious danger of capsize bow over stern

if the boat were driven too hard in rough water, with the long engine shaft, made necessary by the deep V floor, adding to this risk. It was nonetheless capable of higher speeds, 24 knots, than any other inflatable craft of the time. The hull was filled with polystyrene with the result that a holed hull had little impact on performance. X1 underwent trials with the RNLI in 1965. Desmond Hoare warned that she had been built largely by students '*more skilled with their pens than their hands*'. She was reported on adversely. She had however the distinction of being demonstrated to the Duke of Edinburgh on his visit in 1964. She was later given a Viking funeral, set alight and launched crewless and aflame into the Bristol Channel.

X2 was begun in March 1965. She had a pure deep V shape with 16 degrees deadrise and a blunt bow. The two new developments were that, for the first time, the tube (an enlarged Dunlop Gemini tube) was with difficulty adapted to the wooden hull design, and she was the first College craft to have wheel steering. She achieved a top speed of 28 knots, powered by two 40 hp outboards. The RNLI tried her out too but were unhappy with her violent deceleration when coming over a wave and descending into the trough. Their development team at Gorleston added a false bow for more lift but remained unhappy. Another Viking funeral!

X3 was not a College design and the hull was not built at the College. The Duke of Edinburgh had pressed the RNLI to look at an unusual concept, an adaptation of the catamaran, and the College merely added the tube to the hull which was built in nearby Barry. It was rumoured that some £10,000 had been spent on the design research. This boat, named the **Hydrocar**, was designed by Charles Vintner, the Managing Director of Hydro-Cushion Consultants of London. She was intended to plane like a Hovercraft but on a cushion of water, not air, thereby minimising the hostile effects of tide and current, and to become the world's first hydro-cushion inshore lifeboat. She had twin 40 hp engines. Test runs off the College foreshore showed her capable of speeds up to 25 knots with a

ABOVE LEFT: *HRH The Duke of Edinburgh, from the outset a convinced supporter of the College, examines the boats on his first visit.*

ABOVE RIGHT: *A canoe-rolling demonstration on the same visit.*

fairly comfortable ride in good conditions, but there were serious problems. The tubes were sited too low to allow proper trimming of the rigid hull. Even long-shaft outboard engines were too high to function effectively, and the design failed. It was nonetheless confirmation of two things – rapidly developing interest in the rigid-hulled inflatable, and the College's reputation and role in the field.

The breakthrough was X4, built in the summer of 1966, the first truly successful hollow rigid-floor inflatable. Originally powered by a 40 hp Evinrude, she later achieved 30 knots with a 50 hp Mercury outboard. In overall length 17 feet with a 13 foot 6 inch wooden hull, flat underwater from bow to stern and with wheel steering, she became the College's most reliable and seaworthy rescue boat to date. New, flexible fuel tanks, neatly accommodated in the space on deck beneath the curve of the tubes, were also an immense improvement on old-fashioned metal tanks that were so difficult to stow safely. Her flat underwater shape enabled her to stand upright on shore and on her trolley and to plane well, but she hammered badly against the waves. But X4, featuring the bonding of a relatively high-performance hull with the flexible tube, made accessible to inshore rescue boat design for the first time the experience of the powerboat world. Given tubes adapted to new hull design, there need henceforward be no immediate constraint on power, size or speed. It was a turning point, but not the last.

This well-worn tube shows the first and very basic example of wheel steering and a seat for the helmsman.

Other significant advantages of all these developments now became clear.

Seaworthiness and the safety of the crew had long been key priorities for the RNLI. Speed, always important but in offshore operation quite clearly in second place to safety, was becoming a critical factor with the new demands of inshore rescue. Space for crew and casualties was a real problem in the small traditional inflatable, as were the issues of protection from exposure and the need for some height above sea level when searching for casualties. The small inflatables were tiller-driven from a low position, and the crew members sat uncomfortably on the bouncing tubes, holding on as best they could in rough seas. 'Tube riding' was one of the excitements for the Atlantic College students, but they were rarely at sea for more than an hour or two in the afternoon, and their normal patrol and rescue area was generally the limited bay between St Donat's and Llantwit Major. The introduction of the firm wooden floor now made it possible to install saddle seats which were ridden rather as one rides a horse, gripping firmly with the knees and with the feet inserted in foot straps glued to the floor, eyes and hands free to roam and to work independently and from a higher position, thus greatly increasing the range of observation. These seats were suitable for two or three crew members. They provided the natural location for the steering wheel and remote controls for the outboard engine. The resulting weight distribution gave the boat better balance in all conditions except a following sea, when it was desirable to have more weight aft. Fatigue was also long postponed. The floor provided good space for casualties and even for stretchers. Masts could be erected for radio antennae and for navigation and search lights, thus bringing closer night operation for the first time in the history of inflatable rescue craft. The seats themselves provided locker space for auxiliary equipment. The inflatable was becoming a true lifeboat.

ABOVE LEFT: *All new boats were given a champagne launch.*

ABOVE RIGHT: *The long slog from the low tide mark back to the slipway and the workshops!*

CHAPTER 5
The Opening of the Atlantic College RNLI Station and Early Rescues

In its first summer, 1963, the College had begun acting as a rescue centre, called out in June to a search off Llantwit Major and in August on a similar errand for a missing person, believed drowned, who reappeared three weeks later in Blackpool, having suffered memory loss.

Looking back, it seems natural that the College should have become one of the first of the RNLI inshore lifeboat stations. At the time, it was not so clear. However, in March 1964 the College took official responsibility for the roughly 22-mile stretch of Bristol Channel coastline between Barry, 10 miles to the east, and Porthcawl, 12 miles to the north west, the first RNLI auxiliary lifeboat station ever to be run by a school or university in Britain, probably worldwide, and one of the first nine overall to have been established. The students who manned the boats were thus able to be registered as the youngest crew members so far in the history of the RNLI. It was an example to be followed later in many other stations.

The first rescue came almost immediately, an important and an exciting moment. On Sunday 15th March 1964 a dinghy was reported in distress at 16.42 between Porthcawl and Southerndown Beach, some ten miles distant.

It had been a fine spring afternoon with sunshine until about 13.00 with a moderate north-west wind and spring tides flooding from 14.30, leading to an unusually big swell running onto the College beach at St Donat's. The afternoon's sailing activities were over and most people were in the shower when the call came. Because of the surf and tidal conditions the boats were moved round to Southerndown Beach by road. *Aphrodite* launched first into 8-foot surf at 17.10 with the RNLI Zodiac inflatable following soon after. The Zodiac almost immediately fractured its floor boards and spray deck support and was at reduced speed. A helicopter heard overhead had gone home because of poor visibility. The dinghy had capsized several times. Its occupants were lying exhausted in the bilges and did not see their rescuers until they came alongside. Their chances of survival without rescue were nil. During the landing through surf, one of the casualties was separated from the boat but was quickly recovered by a crew member who brought him in to the shore. This rescue clearly demonstrated the fragility of the standard RNLI inflatable in surf at that time, the value of the skin suit in entering the water to assist, and the importance of familiarity in handling sailing dinghies. In his official report Desmond Hoare also stressed his view that crews of two were insufficient for inshore rescue boats – three was the safe minimum. Had the dinghy been a few hundred yards nearer the cliff face, he argued, it would have become necessary to anchor the rescue boat clear of the breakers and send in a swimmer on a long line.

On 31st May the same year, the College boats rescued two adults who had been cut off by the tide and landed them safely. Exactly one week later they stood by a group, also cut off, until the tide receded and they could make their own way back.

In August came the report of a girl swept out to sea. An RNLI inflatable which had reached the College only the previous evening was launched but suffered a complete collapse of its floor boards in choppy waters off the Nash Sands. It had to return to base. Meanwhile a College boat, driven round to Southerndown by road, was launched from the beach and joined the search for the girl, whose body was eventually recovered from the sea by helicopter.

The same month saw another operation illustrating the potential of fast reaction time and combined operations. The College Cliff Rescue Unit reached a stranded party at the same time as the inshore rescue boat crew. Canoe lifeguards led the rescue boat ashore through the surf, having found the safest route onto the boulder-stricken beach. Meanwhile the Barry Lifeboat had taken two hours to cover the ten miles to St Donat's against the flood tide. The Nash Sands Race was impassable to the College inflatable in rough conditions, and the flexibility afforded by road transport was demonstrated once again.

June 1965 saw the first exploratory use of radio equipment. A young boy who had fallen from the cliffs and broken both wrists was given first aid and brought ashore and thence to hospital. No first aid equipment was specified by the RNLI and the College equipment proved inadequate in quantity. The lack was made up

"I have always found intelligent sailors to be about the most adaptable of all professional men; and to see this retired Rear Admiral – looking exactly like a Welsh Doctor Who in his skin diver's suit running the outdoor side by energetic participation and the indoor side by sympathetic delegation – is to realise that, had he not existed for Atlantic's purposes, he would have had to be invented": Gordon Brook-Shepherd, writing in the *Daily Telegraph* after the College opened.

A well-worn, rather weary tube nonetheless stimulates interest among some of the College's many international visitors.

by the equipment of the second College boat on the scene. Lessons were being learned.

The 10th August 1965 provided another hard lesson. Six people had been cut off by the tide some six miles to the east. The College boats stood by until it became clear that the falling tide offered no danger. In the meantime a capsized canoe some five miles to the north west left one man drowned and two boys who made it safely ashore, the boats delayed by the previous incident. While it was practically certain that no possible action by the College crews could have saved life in view of the distance involved, these overlapping incidents revealed the clear need for more effective radio communication.

The next two years included, among other call-outs, College boats standing by a yacht in distress, persons again cut off by the tide, assistance to a woman who had been removed from the sea by her husband and was lying at the water's edge unconscious, the man with his two small children in a state of helpless panic, Trinity House engineers taken out to the Nash Sands light buoy that had broken down, several false alarms, the recovery of the body of a fisherman who had fallen off the rocks and on whom mouth-to-mouth resuscitation failed, an unsuccessful

40

search for a man reported drowned (the body had however already been brought ashore), assistance given to a capsized powerboat from which three were rescued safely but with the bodies of two adults and a child recovered the following day from the same accident, a pregnant lady who had fallen into the sea, was successfully given resuscitation and taken ashore and thence to hospital, and a man who had fallen from the cliffs, breaking both wrists, who was also successfully brought ashore for transfer to hospital. By July 1967, the College rigid-hulled inflatables were proving capable time and time again, on exercise and on service, of breaking through the 5-foot overfalls off the Nash Sands. At the same time, the long stretches of cliff, the base of which was inaccessible by land for over two miles at high tide, and the frequency of cliff accidents, were making it essential for the boats to carry stretchers. Another lesson learned and now to be implemented!

On 11th November 1968 there came perhaps the most dramatic call-out to date, which also led to the first RNLI Letters of Appreciation to College lifeboat crews. Four men were trapped on a sand dredger wrecked earlier on Tusker Rock off Porthcawl.

Tusker Rock

Tusker Rock had its history. In 1847 there had been two wrecks. The barque **Henry** from Liverpool had struck the reef, eighteen being saved by another vessel, one apprentice drowning. And then the Leith packet bound from Newport for Stirling – all crew again saved by another vessel! On 15th October 1886 the iron ship **Malleney** of Liverpool was thrown on to the Tusker Rock in squalls of hurricane force, in darkness and poor visibility, with the loss of her crew of 20, the first intimation of the tragedy coming when wreckage and six bodies were washed ashore at Nash Point on the night of the 16th. In December 1870 the pilot cutter **The Dasher** struck and was not seen for some time until a momentary break in the fog enabled the Porthcawl Lifeboat to rescue three.

The call-out reached the College at 17.08. Three College-built boats, Xs 4, 5 and 7, were launched in the dark and made their way through difficult seas past the Nash Sands and tidal race, Xs 4 and 7 proceeding five miles on to the wreck site and X5 positioning herself off Nash Point to provide a radio link with the College. X7 had an experimental foot throttle which was disliked by the crew and removed immediately after this service. The report of 18-year-old Willem de Vogel from The Netherlands, the student captain of the Inshore Life Boat Unit, described the scene and included some useful comment on boat and equipment:

> When we arrived … we could see a little fire on the aft deck of the wreck … four men were on board and by shouting at them we came to know that they had lost their little dinghy by which they had boarded the wreck … a very big surf was turning near the wreck and I estimate that the biggest waves were between six and eight feet … we waited for a calm spell and then came alongside very quickly … even though we had

picked the right time we were banged very badly and I credit our success to the fact that our tubes could take the impact of the banging ... three men got on board all right but the fourth one missed and got caught between our tube and the wreck ... the man would have been injured very badly if our boat had been of rigid construction ... Goetz Unger took the men to Ogmore where they were landed through small surf ... I decided to return home as quickly as possible because of the dark ... West of Nash we met X5 ... when we came in sight of the Castle lights we established contact again with the beach party which was very easy to see in their orange anoraks.

From the shore, the boats at sea were barely visible. At the end of the operation the boats were recovered in complete darkness through the 4-foot surf of the rising mid-tide swell. It was a new, deeply satisfying experience. However, the official return of service report to the RNLI Headquarters noted that '*X5 repainted in RNLI colours was almost invisible in the darkness and much less visible than X7 and X4 in AC colours of canary yellow and flame orange*'. Another lesson! For this service, Letters of Appreciation were sent by the RNLI to Goetz Unger from Germany, Willem de Vogel from The Netherlands and Pelham Allen from England. Pelham was 16½ at the time of this rescue and the youngest person then to have received an RNLI Letter of Commendation for life saving at sea.

This rescue had a dismaying sequel. Exactly one week after the College rescue on 11th November 1968, the four rescued men and one additional companion from the same salvage company returned to the wreck in a small dinghy. The dinghy overturned in the heavy swell. Four scrambled back aboard. A fifth, the father of three and one of the four who had been rescued the previous week, was drowned.

CHAPTER 6
Training – the Lighter Side and a Near Disaster

The College response to call-out emergencies was convincing proof of its achievements as an inshore lifeboat station, but its RNLI status reflected more than anything else its pioneering role in boat design and construction. It also stemmed from its innovations in crew training and qualifications. It is interesting to look back at the Guidance for Honorary Secretaries of RNLI Stations dated April 1964:

> *No man who habitually wears glasses is to be enrolled. It is most desirable that members of Inshore Rescue Boats crews should be able to swim, but the lack of a swimming qualification need not debar a man who is in other respects suitable ... inshore rescue boats are not to be used during hours of darkness ... they are for use in conjunction with inshore casualties within five miles of their base ... their use must be restricted to moderate sea conditions corresponding to force five winds ... they are at all times to be manned by a crew of two men ...*

These instructions may have amused Desmond Hoare, who was colour-blind. One assumes that the Royal Navy is not supposed to have admirals who are colour-

High tide launches from the College slipway required the helmsman to clip a lead on to a long line that was anchored off-shore and to haul his boat rapidly clear of the incoming surf.

blind. It is said that, when he was applying for cadet entry to the Navy, there was a helpful uncle on the examining board who pointed out the dials: 'Come on, Desmond. Surely you know that red dials are on the left, green on the right.'

The crew members of the Atlantic College lifeboats used to be briefed by Desmond before their RNLI medical examination in case they were short-sighted: 'Learn the number of the doctor's car by heart – that's all you are asked to look at.' What is certain is that, at sea with the students off St Donat's, he was generally unable to see the shore and relied on the wave direction and student guidance for knowing roughly where he was.

In all other training respects the College was infinitely more stringent.

Amid all the choices, academic and other, open to the College students, only three were truly compulsory: learning to swim, learning to life save, and learning first aid. But would-be crew members and helmsmen for RNLI registration had also to meet additional requirements: in swimming, the Gold Survival Test of the Amateur Swimming Association, the snorkel tests A, B and C of the British Sub-Aqua Club and the Award of Merit of the Royal Life Saving Society; in first aid the Higher Award of the St John Ambulance Brigade; in canoeing the Sea Proficiency Test of the British Canoe Union (the first draft of which had been prepared by the College at a conference held at St Donat's in October 1963); in sailing the Helmsman Test of the Royal Yachting Association; and in rescue boating a series of practical tests in seamanship, rope handling and knots, rowing and theory. One can readily note in these externally assessed skill requirements the precedent for the subsequent introduction by the RNLI of 'competencies' in its enhanced crew training programmes.

Time afloat on the Bristol Channel was underpinned by theory sessions in August. The College had adopted an unusual timetable: two terms of some 20 weeks each, with the second-year students returning in early August to man the rescue services for what was referred to in those days as 'the drowning season'. Every afternoon was given over to intensive training. The rescue boaters began with the early afternoon Shipping Forecast, which was written down, analysed and recalled the following day for a 'post mortem'. There followed an hour by Desmond Hoare on the background to all factors bearing on rescue work at sea for, he said, *'seamanship cannot be learned ashore, and there is no alternative to spending hours and hours at sea if one is going to be safe in boat handling and competent in rescue. Nevertheless, intelligent people usually like to understand some of the theory which underlies their experience, and the theory enriches the experience.'* These lectures covered such matters as boat management and boat handling, equipment, tidal motion and the structure and behaviour of waves, weather, propulsion, inshore rescue and the skills required, the local coastline and navigation, and the principles behind inflatable lifeboat design. They ended with a written examination.

There can be no doubt of their impact. One Danish student 20 years later remembered *'one detail from the section on wave theory that made a very vivid impression on the mind of a 17-year-old. He casually mentioned that he was on duty on a battleship during World War Two, and during a convoy to Murmansk the waves were so huge that the battleship sailed uphill and downhill. I spent the entire night visualising a battleship sailing uphill …'*

BELOW LEFT: *HM The Queen visits in 1965.*

BELOW RIGHT: *Chic Thompson, Director of Activities, and Roger Haslam, physicist and Chief Coach of the Beach Rescue Unit, present the College surf life saving team.*

The Bristol Channel surf rolls in at low tide across the rocky foreshore.

For the rest of the academic year, September to June, sea-going took place every afternoon except Saturday. On a typical day, there might be some 12 Fireball dinghies and perhaps 4 to 6 single-handed Minisail dinghies at sea together with up to 20 canoeists, although the last named prided themselves on being independent of motorised assistance – and being well practised in the techniques of the Eskimo role, their self-confidence was usually well merited. Training exercises up and down the Channel, the frequent need to stand by struggling sailors whilst they righted their capsized craft, the throwing and handling of tow lines, above all the launching and recovery of the rescue boats themselves through surf – often carried out on other parts of the coast in order to gain familiarity with lesser-known areas of the Channel foreshore – and hours of driving the boats in all the conditions of the Bristol Channel, gave the crews real confidence in their skills, their boats and one another. Unsurprisingly, it was all highly motivating and highly enjoyable, with perhaps the one exception of the requirement, insisted on mercilessly by Desmond Hoare, that all crews should learn to right a rescue boat from a capsized position. This was done in February, often in bitterly cold conditions, with a bag of stones strapped to the transom of an otherwise stripped hull to simulate the weight of an engine. Happily, no College rescue boat ever capsized on operations at sea, but these were the days before the RNLI developed crew-activated righting systems, and it was a necessary precaution.

Other events were indisputably more enjoyable – the first ever crossing to Porlock on the Somerset coast with the aim of enabling the Headmaster to travel on to the island of Lundy (the weather turned, the crew were unable to set out on the return journey and spent the evening and night in a local hostelry dressed only in their skin suits); participation in the local powerboat races off nearby Porthcawl for which the student crews were anxious to unload all possible equipment and weight, only to be rebuked sternly by their admiral Headmaster that they were rescue, not racing craft and must never be caught out with their pants down or anchors unstowed; summer picnics on the Nash Sands; and the time when two crews, with Desmond, were marooned on Flatholm Island for a week by bad weather and camped in the abandoned old cholera hospital '*We camped in the bitter cold in the ruined cholera hospital. DJH kept us busy with navigation exercises, firewood gathering, games, etc. He'd brought a seemingly endless supply of Cinzano which we sipped in front of the fire as we listened to naval tales. By the end of the week, even those foreigners who mistrusted his British headmasterly ways had quite warmed up to him*'. There were pre-Christmas boarding parties of the Breaksea Light Vessel, bearing bottles of whisky and other seasonal gifts for the crew. One Dutch student of the first generation remembers making tight high-speed turns in **Bacchus** with Desmond aboard. Desmond slipped and there were some strange cracking noises. Before supper that night, this student was called to the Headmaster's sitting room and told by Naomi that he had broken three of Desmond's ribs. The student was offered supper on two conditions – that he would not make Desmond laugh because that would hurt, and that he would not tell anyone else because that would make them laugh.

Desmond Hoare was thought, rightly, to be ready to do anything to raise money for his rescue boats. When a barge carrying several valuable mahogany trees overturned in the Channel, the students were immediately sent out to try and find them. The public service justification was to remove an obvious hazard to shipping, but the glint in Desmond's eye when he was quizzed about salvage rights told another story. As luck would have it, the fog came down and they wallowed around unsuccessfully in the pea soup with the Nash foghorn apparently coming from all directions at once. On the second afternoon visibility improved and they actually found a log. Desmond Hoare hammered a screwdriver into it and made fast a line, but it was so heavy and so low in the water that **Atalanta** simply could not tow it fast enough to beat the tide. Very reluctantly they had to let it go. The summer after leaving the College, one of the students who had taken part in the log search was working for a fisherman in Lynmouth on the Devon shore of the Channel. This fisherman told him of the day when, some months earlier, he had found a mahogany log at sea, towed it home, and been puzzled to find a screwdriver embedded in one end.

Black Thursday

But things did not always go well, and Thursday 28th October 1965 entered the College annals as 'Black Thursday'. Two RNLI inflatables and the College's **Aphrodite** were at sea with four Fireball sailing dinghies one afternoon when a large swell developed suddenly from the west as the tide turned and the wind freshened. After one dinghy got into difficulties in breaking surf, **Aphrodite** lost the use of her engine when attempting to assist and was compelled to anchor. She was recovered and towed ashore by a second rescue boat, but by this time all four Fireballs were in difficulties and capsizing repeatedly. A third College boat, **Bacchus**, was launched and managed to recover and bring ashore one Fireball and its crew. Two Fireballs were ordered to anchor at sea and had their crews taken off. By now one of the RNLI boats had also lost the use of its engine and was anchored, its crew recovered safely. By the time the last boat and crew were ashore, there was breaking water on the crest of nearly every wave. Two of the Fireballs were later recovered from the rocks, badly damaged, having dragged their anchors. The third was lost. During the night, the anchored rescue boat was also driven ashore, its nylon warp having parted, finishing up by good fortune on a sandy spit from where it and its engine were secured the following morning with only minor damage. It was the nearest the College ever came to real disaster, a severe reminder of the fatefully narrow dividing line between sound adventurous activity and unforeseen tragedy. The official return submitted by the College to RNLI Head Office recorded nine lives saved. Desmond Hoare, no doubt strengthened by years of professional naval experience, held his nerve in a manner that no civilian colleague could have done. Life went on as before.

Underlying his confidence was an acute consciousness of the importance of safety review. Only six months after this near-miss occasion, he was writing a long and confidential paper for the Chairman of Outward Bound, who was also a member of the College governing body, on the principle of independent investigation. His two main points were the necessity of recognising the significance of 'near-misses' and the absolute need for the committee of enquiry to include a representative or representatives of the national or statutory body responsible for the sport in question. Scarcely less important was the need for these bodies to maintain exact records and to make them available annually to the press. The RNLI Inshore Rescue Boat Return Form was, he wrote, a model of completeness and lucidity, as indeed it is, and could give other organisations some helpful guidance. Only complete compliance with the rules laid down by the proper national authorities could lead to support from them if and when accidents or near-misses occurred. In the incident described above, a detailed report was submitted to the RNLI, who decided that no follow-up action was called for.

CHAPTER 7

Further Innovations, a Breakthrough with the RNLI, and the Workshop Experience

The College was now making a name for itself in the wider marine world. The 1966 Boat Show at Earls Court had an Atlantic College rigid-hulled inflatable on display. It was intensively photographed by excited Japanese business scouts.

The next two craft, X5 and X6, were a pair. Started in June 1967, they were 18 feet in overall length with a rigid hull of 15 feet 6 inches and an increased beam, and were fitted with extended Dunlop Gemini tubes. The underwater lines were derived directly from X4 and were flat almost from bow to stern but with some V shape in the bow to lessen the hammering against the waves. The tubes were raised relative to the hull to ensure that they remained clear of the water when under power, thus producing far less drag. Equipped with 50 hp Mercury engines, they had a top speed of 34 knots, a major advance on the performance of the standard RNLI inflatable boat of 22.5 knots with a 40 hp engine. Perhaps even more significantly, there was twice the space for casualties and far greater comfort and visibility for the crew – this proved especially important with X5 which, not long after its first launch, had rescued an expectant mother from drowning. The hollow rigid floor, thanks to its box structure, was inherently very strong indeed and almost maintenance free, although extensive sea-going led to failure of some of the longitudinal joints in the skin. Although not structural, these cracks allowed water to enter, and the problem was cured by taping rubber strips along the joints. The whole floor, including ribs and the outer skin, was made of ³/₈ inch marine plywood, held together by glue and an impressive number of screws and brass bolts, and weighed just 145 kg (320 lb). X5 had an operational range of around 75 miles. Her active and ambitious builders and crew, Paul Jefferies from Britain and Martti Salomaa from Finland, were allowed to enter her in the 50 hp class of the Porthcawl Powerboat Race that year and finished second in competition with what they later described as 'very hot machinery'.

Stimulated not only by this exciting success but also by Desmond Hoare's tolerant, indeed active, encouragement of student initiative, Paul Jefferies went on to build a second boat of his own design, modifying the underwater shape in an effort to reduce pounding and to keep the bow down. Alas, his decision to have one longitudinal frame only, albeit with considerable lateral bracing, was

Desmond Hoare and students 'messing about in boats'.

*Paul Jefferies' **Glory-
A-B** a few minutes
before she broke her back.*

fatal. The first time full throttle was applied and the boat had reached over 35 knots there was a Big Bang! The forward third of the boat had folded back at right angles. The crew jumped overboard and the boat was left quivering in the water. She had broken her back, and the only thing that kept her together was the inflatable tube. Desmond Hoare was not amused. The failure of a design experiment he took in his stride, but the firing of a flare for assistance, and the consequent call from HM Coastguard for rescue, was another matter.

Happily for Paul Jefferies' pride, a mould had been taken, and Geoffrey Jones from the USA took the lead in the College's first entirely student-inspired venture into fibre glass (GRP) construction. The result was a solid but heavy boat, X10, whose internal polystyrene buoyancy eventually became thoroughly waterlogged. Great difficulties were experienced in bonding the tube to the glass fibre, and an unsatisfactory compromise was attempted with an intervening wooden strip. It was a brave attempt, but the workshop resources and expertise were inadequate for this kind of work.

Meanwhile, X5 had been loaned to the RNLI for six months of trials at Lyme Regis. The reports from highly experienced lifeboat men there were impressively encouraging. It was clear that they were being offered something very new – and very challenging. Extracts from their reports make this clear:

Under heavy conditions [in the Portland Race], the distance between crests was not much more than a boat's length so that the bow was on the back of one breaking sea and the stern lifting in front of the following breaking sea ... maintaining control was not difficult but required extreme caution and continual throttle control ... in moderate conditions [there is] a marked tendency to become airborne at all speeds ... running before a sea this boat tends to bury her head when she overtakes one [wave] and runs

Endless rubber scraping!

into the back of the sea ahead ... X5 also had the extra power and manoeuvrability to take advantage of any gaps in the wave patterns and to accelerate out of trouble, especially when running before a heavy sea. In fact on a number of the later runs through the Race, conditions were such that I would not have voluntarily taken an IRB into them even for trials ... it would have been foolhardy to have entered it with an IRB, yet in this boat I had every confidence ... this boat requires far more concentration and control than the standard IRB as there is very little room for error whereas with the IRB most mistakes are got away with ... training of a crew for this craft would require keener selection and care ... driving into and obliquely to the seas, full speed was unbearable and dangerous ... running before the seas anything could be negotiated bearing in mind the speed and quick response to the throttle ... it must be stressed that this boat requires more care and concentration from its helmsman. Under adverse conditions these qualities are essential, much more so than in an IRB ... we have these men and I recommend that station trials continue at Lyme to obtain experience under service conditions ...

There were still important lessons to be learned. Crew sitting on the tubes ('tube-riding') were at risk at speed in heavy seas. The type and position of the throttle required modification to enable more sensitive control. Above all, and this had long been a problem, the hull had a strong tendency to bury its bow in the trough of the wave ahead when moving at speed in a following sea. X5 returned to the College after the six months with the tube becoming detached at the bow from the rigid hull.

The constructional methods at the College were now producing strong and thoroughly reliable hulls, able to withstand all that the Bristol Channel had to offer, both at sea and when returning to its rocky shores.

There was also the intimate and direct relationship between the sea-going experience and the workshop experience:

the incredible atmosphere ... a permanent smell of glue and thinners and wood shavings ... endless scratching of rubber strips with hacksaw blades to get a good key for the glue ... the heady smell of the glue itself (why did none of us get hooked on it?) ... Cascamite wood glue mixed in yogurt pots at the sink ... heavy applications of steam from an electric kettle to persuade the timber to conform to the required shape ... all of Saturdays and Sundays were spent at the workshops as if it were some kind of ritual ... one always left covered from head to toe in dust ... unending discussions about deep V-hulls and spray rails ... one had the feeling that experiments were being tried out all the time.

The dependence of successful and safe sea-going on successful and conscientious workmanship ashore was transparent. The discipline of the situation was speaking for itself, and *'the thing got hold of us to a consuming degree'*. And there was as well *'the great camaraderie that came from having to work together, although sometimes the people were as challenging as the weather'*. One former student wrote: *'The lessons in team building and engineering are of use daily as I send out small teams designing and installing nuclear safety equipment.'* The materials were high quality mahogany marine ply, large quantities of brass screws and bolts, spruce fillets shaped and moulded with the use of steam kettles to fit the curves of the longitudinal ribs, the complete avoidance of electrical drills to eliminate hasty and careless work, the use of slow-setting glues to ensure precision and attention to detail.

Many efforts were made by students impatient for faster results to find more rapid ways of preparing the rubber surfaces for gluing, but none proved more effective than hours of laborious work roughening up surfaces with broken-off hacksaw blades and repeated preparatory coats of thinned glue before the relevant surfaces were 'mated' together. Bob Hale had been a cobbler before he joined the College maintenance staff; hence the use of the shoemakers' glue Gripsolite in building the boats. One student spoke for many when he recalled *'The smell of the glue was all-pervading and stuck to hands and clothes in an unforgiving way.'* And Desmond Hoare used to tell them: *'You are no use until you can smell the difference between copper and brass in the dark.'*

Desmond rarely set out designs on paper. His view was *'if it looks right, it is right'* – not a world away from the principle that the more beautiful the equation, the more likely it is to be accurate, which led the British physicist Paul Dirac to the concept of anti-matter and a Nobel Prize. All the hulls were built upside down on cradles, or jigs, sometimes the same one for successive craft – Xs 9 to 12, for example. The longitudinal frames or bulkheads were made from plywood with spruce stringers bolted on to the extremities and made oversize to enable them to be cut back to their final shape. Dozens of pieces of string were tightened over the frames laterally time and again to check whether the longitudinal frames, widened on their edges with the spruce stringers, were planed to the correct angle to ensure that the plywood skin was in full contact with the longitudinal frame over its full length. This was the critical stage. In this manner too the final underwater shape was defined. Roy Thomas, who spent three years in the boat workshops, said *'DJH knew by eye'*. There was no circular saw (too much risk of injuries with inexperienced student operators), no electric drill. All was done by hand. Pump screwdrivers were used for the innumerable screws. Araldite, the early epoxy glue, was forbidden – it set too quickly. The monthly

Constructing a rubber seat for one of the early boats. These seats were glued to the tubes to provide greater comfort and height above sea level for better observation.

consumption of the wood glue Cascamite was around 13 kg (28 lb). The working aprons became stiff and stood up by themselves.

It was, in the words of another student recalling Desmond Hoare and the boats, '*the art of his eye and hand that translated them into reality*'. Desmond sought little credit for himself. His students, with some justice, thought him rather autocratic, but he was at heart a listener and an observer. Writing years earlier about Outward Bounding in the Royal Navy, he had speculated about the voyage of HMS *Beagle*: '*I can imagine some Naval officer, listening to Charles Darwin, pouring out his thoughts one evening on the multiplicity and inter-relationships of life, and saying: "It's like a great tidal stream"; and then the genius getting to work on the chance remark.*' He was much later to say that the boats were '*designed by the Bristol Channel with the midwives of trial and error and 500 students as development officers*'.

Martti Salomaa from Finland remembered: '*In our mind's eye we can still vividly visualise "Des" in his worn-out blue sweatshirt, contemplating design with the glint of enthusiasm in his eyes, and with his huge pipe between his teeth; he would nod his head thoughtfully, and he was always so keenly interested to muse over ideas that the pipe was in a constant need of replenishment – that's Des'igning!!!*' The key fact is that the students were full partners in the whole enterprise.

Boats also needed trolleys, and teamwork in the beach parties was a key element in ensuring safety in the critical moments of launch and recovery, both in the surf on the beach and, even more so, in heavy swell on the slipway itself, bordered by treacherous rocks. At the very beginning, the rescue boats were carried down to the water's edge and the engines fitted there before launching. Before long, trolleys made of alloy tubes and simple wheels with tyres made this carrying unnecessary. But the need to keep the long trolley handles on the beach side made it necessary to lift and turn the boats before the next day's sea-going. As boat weight increased, this became impracticable. Again the solution, once adopted, seemed obvious – open-ended reversible trolleys. All rescue boaters and sailors will remember hauling the boats up the slipway – a steep haul and a long one at low tide. Desmond Hoare would not allow a winch as student fingers were precious and he wanted none lost through inexperience with the use of mechanical gear. Return to the trolley, in surf and above all on the steeply sloping slipway, required careful and precise judgement from the helmsman and split-second teamwork from the crew responsible for lifting the engine promptly as the trolley was recovered from the water. Just occasionally, a boat would overrun – a moment of great potential danger for the beach party – and the engines were eventually equipped with cut-off cords to enable the coxswain to judge the moment with absolute precision. A successful return was always a very satisfying experience, as Carl Erik Benzinger from Denmark was happy to recall: '*Precisely at the moment when the swell surged past the trolley, I cut the engine, settling the boat down squarely on the trolley as though guided by a laser … it was a euphoric moment. I had mastered my craft!*'

Commercial Developments

By this stage the College was deriving growing benefit from the active interest and support of the Avon Rubber Company and especially its general manager, Tom Norreys. Tom, formerly in the Merchant Navy, was to become Chairman of the Ship and Boat Builders National Federation Export Committee and a Committee member of the Marine Traders Association. He had been responsible for inflatables from the moment that Avon entered the market in 1959. The company, known until then only for its tyres, was exploring the market for small inflatables as yacht tenders. Their first products, the 8-foot Redstart and the 12-foot Redshank dinghies, were exhibited at the London Boat Show in 1960. Avon claims then to have pioneered the inflatable for the pleasure market in both the UK and the USA. Their rapid market growth is illustrated by the following sales figures: 1960 – 255; 1961 – 780; 1962 – 1,400; 1963 – 1,800.

Their original intention had been less the leisure market than an attempt to prove to the Ministry of Defence that they could make satisfactory inflatables and thereby get on to the government's tender list for life rafts, inflatable boats and life jackets. Before long they introduced the wooden transom craft called Rovers with stub tubes aft of the transom to support larger engines, and they moved from there to larger craft capable of handling engines up to 40–50 hp. It was Desmond Hoare who pressed them to build stronger and thicker floors as their tubes were already outliving at least three floors. At the 1967 London Boat Show they displayed a 4-metre boat with a wooden rigid hull but aroused little interest. That year they sold 30 to 40 craft but had problems with leaking hulls. It was then that Norreys met the glass-fibre boat builder Stewart Galt and entered into a joint agreement. Galt had already built a large rigid-hulled inflatable he called the Raider. This later became the Avon-Galt Sea Rider, a 4-metre hull with quite a deep V (*'the boat for going out when others were coming in'*, Norreys called it). They went to the London and Paris boat shows in 1968 with these craft – a good success in London, but in Paris the police took the boat off the stand and locked it away on the grounds that it infringed a French patent! A Frenchman had, it transpired, visited St Donat's and taken out a national patent on the fixing of the inflatable tube to the hull, copying exactly the methods used at the College. Although the French patent was dated after the showing and selling of their first Riders, Avon lost the case and were banned from selling in France for 21 years. It must have been some consolation that, the following year, they took orders worth over £60,000 and exported some 1,000 boats to the United States.

The Avon fabric was of the highest quality – heavy duty nylon with a tensile strength of some 350 lb per inch and a tear strength of 70–80 lb per inch width. It was coated on each side with a synthetic rubber compound that provided the air-keeping property of the material and protected the nylon fabric from chafe. Rigorous provision was also made for resistance to ageing, ultra-violet light discoloration, sea water, oil and low temperature and even the effects of ozone deterioration. Their standards for life rafts were three times more stringent than those set by the Board of Trade. Tom Norrey's willingness now to have tubes made according to College designs was a vital, indeed fundamental, factor in the final emergence of the rigid-hulled inflatable as a major new rescue craft.

The Final Innovation – the Removal of the Transom

It was the two craft X7 and X8 that brought the last really critical innovation in development towards the final design. Work began in June 1968. For the first time the hulls were designed independently of ready-made tubes, the tubes being made up by Avon to Desmond Hoare's specifications. Smaller than their immediate predecessors and measuring 16 feet 6 inches overall with hulls of 13 feet 9 inches, these two boats had identical hulls with a deeper V at the bow and a flat run aft. Both boats were again equipped with 50 hp Mercury engines and achieved speeds in excess of 30 knots despite their shorter length. Experimentation took place over the size, shape and location of the driving 'saddle', one unfruitful and acutely uncomfortable attempt being made to place it right up in the bow for better visibility. The foot throttle was another unsuccessful and short-lived experiment. Drawing on the practices of the Surf Life Saving Association, a swimming reel and line were added and became standard equipment in all future boats. But the most important innovation was the dramatically successful removal of a large part of the transom.

Operating in and out of surf almost every day, the College boats were all too often weighed down and impeded in their manoeuvrability when filled with water.

This shot of X7 shows her clear lines and is a fine example of the increasingly expert student craftsmanship. It also shows the flexible fuel tanks that were now stowed in the space between the tube and the hull floor and the unpopular helmsman's position in the bow and the unsuccessful foot throttle. The stub transom allows water taken aboard to flow unimpeded and rapidly over the stern. This was the final major breakthrough in design.

The art of hand and eye.

The self-draining arrangements were clumsy and slow. Thanks to the depth of the rigid hull in these new boats, the floor was now above the water line. Even when power was suddenly cut off, the following surge of water failed to rise to the floor level. It was suddenly clear that the transom was needed only to support the engine. From X7 and X8 onwards, all engines were mounted on a narrow central pillar constructed of several layers of marine ply, firmly anchored to the inner longitudinal ribs of the hull by oak knees. The boats had now gained a real surf capability, being able to run along or away from the waves and choose the moment to climb out seawards. Rapid and total self-draining in surf had transformed their operational potential. Long shaft engines were also important because they raised the power head a useful 5 inches higher than the water sweeping out of the boat over the stern after flooding in surf.

X7 was loaned to the RNLI for trials and was fitted with a 55 hp Evinrude. The criticisms were outweighed by much approval. To their report that she was unable to remain horizontal in a short steep sea, Desmond Hoare observed drily: *'Not surprising for a water length of less than 14 foot at 30 knots.'* The RNLI wanted more length for greater security, although neither boat had ever showed any sign of capsizing at sea.

X8 was driven around the south coast in the Plymouth/Portsmouth area by its two student builders, Willem de Vogel from The Netherlands and Luc Celt from the United States, in the summer of 1968, arousing great interest wherever it went. They lived in a tent off a beach and always anchored the boat in a cove at night. Soon after setting up camp they noticed a marine in a Zodiac, always doing the same crossing of Plymouth Harbour at predictable times. *'We soon started hunting him and turning circles round him and spraying him.'*

The Changing RNLI

By the mid-1960s, the growth in the numbers and activities of the inshore lifeboats was creating some new challenges in public relations for the Royal National Lifeboat Institution. Not only was it rarely possible now to feature those truly heroic and iconic coxswain personalities and crews who had for years dominated the headlines in shipwreck disasters. It was somehow less convincing to be going to the rescue of scores of people, almost always in very small groups if not alone, who had got themselves into trouble all too often by foolishness and ignorance, and in their leisure time, rather than whilst earning their living and confronting danger in their professional lives. There were fewer press pictures too of those magnificent lifeboats crashing down the slipway in a cloud of spray as they set out into stormy oceans! There was another development too, surely a positive sign of the times. It fell to the Atlantic College to play the leading role.

Every autumn, Desmond Hoare sent his list of student names to the RNLI Head Office for registration as official crew members. In October 1968 he found himself with 24 suitably qualified students rather than the more usual number of about 12. This was not however the main issue. One of them was Elisabeth Hostvedt.

Desmond addressed himself to Mr M. S. Porcher, the Assistant Secretary, on 16th October: *'I should perhaps consult you as a matter of principle before putting her name forward. Is this going to be acceptable? There are quite a number of girls who will be qualifying in a year's time and the issue is quite important for us too.'*

Mr Porcher's immediate, personal and unofficial reply was attractively encouraging: *'I can say here and now that my personal view is that I see no reason why a fully qualified*

Elisabeth Hostvedt at the helm, her younger sister Kristin handling radio equipment.

Norwegian girl should not be a member of the IRB crew, and that if I was also a fully qualified crew member I should be positively enthusiastic!' His formal reply followed a few days later and was more guarded:

> The question of having a girl as an IRB crew member is a rather more difficult one. It is not a practice which we would like to see adopted generally because, although a girl might make just as good a helmsman as a boy, in the majority of cases it is problematic whether she would have the strength and the stamina to stand up to a really severe service and to haul a heavy person out of the sea ... We are, however, prepared to make a special case of Elisabeth Hostvedt provided she can pass the full medical test which is required for IRB crew membership, and that you are in all respects satisfied that she has the physique to stand up to an arduous service. For the time being I think we shall have to work on the basis of dealing with each case on its merits ...

Thus the RNLI acquired its first ever female registered crew at an inshore lifeboat station. Elisabeth was at least the granddaughter of an admiral, a Norwegian one. In 1969 she was invited to open the Birmingham Boat Show and her mini-skirt won the RNLI some unusual new headlines. One newspaper, however, the *Caernarvon and Denbigh Herald*, clearly preferred tradition: '*Women, it seems, seep in wherever the boat isn't tightly caulked.*'

In 1971 another female College student, Penny Sutton from Britain, appears to have been the first fully registered RNLI woman crew member to be engaged in an inshore lifeboat service call-out.

Patricia Mucklow was the first female crew member of an all-weather lifeboat crew when she joined the Mallaig Station in 1961, but the inshore lifeboats were now making possible a rapidly growing female participation in active lifeboat work round the British coast.

CHAPTER 8

The Growing Case for Coast Rescue by Teenagers

By the mid-1960s there was no doubt about the growing status and author-ity of both the College and Desmond Hoare in the world of sea and coastal rescue. On average, one quarter of College students elected each year to enrol in the Rescue Boat Corps. The others chose either the Beach Rescue Unit or the Cliff Rescue Unit. The aim was to create comprehensive rescue cover for sea, beach and cliff.

This single-minded emphasis on rescue training (the now far more common forms of community service had started on a modest scale and were to develop strongly later) was the most loyal possible reflection of the Kurt Hahn philosophy:

> William James has challenged statesmen and educators to discover the moral equiva-lent to war. It has been discovered: the passion of rescue releases the highest dynamics of the human soul … he who trains, drills, accepts labours, boredom and danger, all to be ready to help his brother, discovers God's purpose in his inner life and flares up in anger when he encounters the doctrines which despise human life and dignity.

But it was Desmond Hoare, who had first seen young men engaged in rescue work on Australian beaches as a boy, who recognised the practical needs and who seized the practical opportunities.

In an article published in September 1964, written jointly with the College's medical officer, Derek Llewellyn, Desmond had drawn attention to the Report of the Working Party on Accident Prevention and Life Saving of the Royal College of Surgeons, 1961–1963. Here, accidents on the roads, in the home, in industry and in sport had been described as *the modern plague* – 20,000 deaths, 300,000 hospital admissions and 6 million outpatients every year. The article called for training in first aid and life saving to become part of what is commonly known in the school curriculum as health education.

Of the College he wrote, well aware that its public image was too narrowly focused on its outdoor activities*: 'The rescue service activity is unusual, but does not take much time. It gives great pleasure, and it contributes fundamentally to our idea that the quality of the human individual matters more than colour, race, politics or religion.'*

The 'Beach Rescuers' were trained in the techniques of the Amateur Swimming Association (Personal Survival Tests), the Royal Life Saving Society and the Surf Life Saving Association. They learned the 'reel' drills of the Australians in order to be able to recover drowning persons off surf beaches and to handle surf skis and, in many cases, also canoes, becoming qualified members of the British Canoe Union's Corps of Canoe Life Guards. They were on patrol on the local beaches every afternoon from late July until early September and took part with repeated success in the annual Championships of the British Surf Life Saving Association.

The College Cliff Rescue Unit winches a casualty and rescuer in harness up the crumbling cliff face.

The Cliff Rescue Unit faced exceptional problems with the acutely dangerous nature of the crumbling Bristol Channel cliffs. These are related in detail in the account written after he left the College by their first leader, Peter Jolley, the College's senior scientist and Director of Studies, which is given as Appendix 2.

The key innovation was the construction of a flexible crane that projected over the edge of the cliff to avoid the danger of disturbing the face of the crumbling cliff and dispatching rocks and rubble down on the victim. The rescuer was lowered down the cliff face, accompanied by a stretcher in which the victim was then hauled up to safety. Anchors screwed into the ground well back from the cliff edge held everyone and everything in place but could have done little for Jon Whitely, one of the first generation of students and rather well known nationally for the

Other Activities at the College

Whilst the Cliff Rescue Unit with its newly designed, innovative and well-tested crane and associated equipment and techniques had become an auxiliary Coastguard station, the Beach Rescue Unit concentrated on strengthening its skills in handling surf skis and canoes and in competing with great success in the annual Surf Life Saving Championships. The hand-rolling of canoes, achieved by some of the more expert with a single hand, stimulated unfailing enthusiasm in successive generations of students and led to some spectacular sessions of surfing on days of wild weather off the College foreshore. Canoe looping, the deliberate digging-in of the bow as the wave broke, followed by a somersault as the canoe rose into a vertical position before landing usually upside down but just occasionally, with a twist of the body, upright, became the aspiration of the most skilful. The hardened canoeists were of course unfailingly scornful of fellow sea-goers who lived off noisy and smelly engines and spent their time in physically inactive if uncomfortably cold circumstances.

The surfing accomplishments of the canoeists led Desmond Hoare to dream up a four-man canoe with which, so he suggested, an expert team might ride the green waves of the Channel after a storm in unbroken motion from St Donat's right up to Barry — an almost Faustian wager to achieve perpetual motion. It did not work, but the early practices in the swimming pool to coordinate the efforts of the four upside-down canoeists in righting their craft before venturing out into

the Channel provoked some enjoyable entertainment for spectators, and indeed for the Duke of Edinburgh when he performed the naming ceremony on his visit in 1964.

Another short-lived experiment was the project for a rigid-hulled inflatable surf boat whose aim of catching the waves was to be achieved by vigorous team paddling. The specification was:

Length 28 feet, beam 7 feet, weight 520 lbs. The main polystyrene-filled floor will be joined flexibly to a foredeck and a poop deck. 12 paddlers, six a side, and a steersman on the poop deck using a special oar. The poop will have a stabilising fin. It should be able to ride over a six-foot breaker and should surf at speed ... the cost of this boat is being borne by the RNLI as an experimental vehicle for saving life on beaches, especially surf beaches, where powered craft are of little value. If successful, many others will no doubt be built.

It was not and none were! A later version ended up with an outboard engine mounted inboard. The tube surrounded the entire floor; the engine was installed not too far off mid-ships; and this strange rubber monster, topped with a tall tower, served for a time as an admirable admiral's platform for marine photography.

role he had played in the film *Kidnapped*, who was wandering round the cliff top cutting away brambles without having fastened his personal safety rope. He was called back from the edge in soft whispers as though nothing were amiss – it was no doubt as narrow an escape for the College's then embryonic rescue services as for Jon himself.

By 1965, the year in which the Cliff Rescue Unit was recognised as an auxiliary Coastguard station and supplied with a complete range of appropriate equipment to supplement the specialist equipment of its own design, 600 individual National Certificates or Awards in rescue service skills were held by the 154 students in the College.

As early as April 1964, the College had felt ready to hold a conference on Coast Rescue Services in the county of Glamorgan. Attended by representatives of the RNLI, HM Coastguard, RAF Mountain Rescue, the British Canoe Union, the St John Ambulance Brigade, the Central Council of Physical Recreation, many local councils and the Chief Constable of the Glamorgan County Police, this meeting concluded that

> *upwards of one thousand teenagers – boys and girls – could be fully committed to Coast Rescue in Glamorgan. This suggests at least twenty-five times that number for Britain as a whole, the engagement of twenty-five thousand young people to save the lives of some five hundred a year; each of these twenty-five thousand would have acquired First Aid and Life Saving skills which they could also use in the home, in industry and on the roads, where so many accidents occur. As parents, they would be likely in later life to encourage their children to acquire similar qualifications.*

After this meeting, Desmond Hoare consulted the Presidents of the British Canoe Union and the British Surf Life Saving Association. He wrote:

> *If the RNLI decides to encourage the manning of the Inshore Rescue Boat crews with teenagers, as the Atlantic College has shown to be entirely practicable, the potential teenage involvement in 1968 might be approximately 1000. Such involvement would require a training facility for instructors in the Inshore Rescue Boat skills … this service demands a comprehensive set of skills and is particularly appropriate to Sea Scouts, Sea Cadets and Cadet members of yacht clubs … the various Coast Rescue Services have grown up piecemeal and there is a considerable task of co-ordination waiting to be done over matters such as recruiting and training, signals and combined unit rescue procedures …*

And of course he pressed the College case: '*The College is the only place in Britain presenting a fully coordinated Coast Rescue Service manned entirely by teenagers and safeguarding ten miles of coast.*'

A few weeks later, Desmond Hoare was following up a meeting with the Minister at the Department of Science and Education with a letter to him:

As we see it, there is a real need for a focal point in Britain for teenage coast rescue development, and the Atlantic College fits this need ... there is a virtually unlimited demand for training of young teachers, youth leaders, police cadets, etc., and our training facilities are only part used ... there are some who are surprised that an all-sixth form international school, preparing boys for universities, should regard this development as one in which to play a part. Others see that our high academic intent is exactly the reason why we should seek, not just a part, but a leading part in a development affecting the human attitudes of youth at large. It is right that the brightest boys should be those most deeply committed in human affairs and that in their education they should share some of the resources given to them ...

He went on: '*It has been customary in this country to foster school cadet corps as pre-service training for the Armed Forces. New ideas are emerging ... one prime educational aim in schools and youth organisations today should be the generation of a spirit of helpfulness.*' He called for the setting up of a National Coast Rescue Steering Committee. But for the next year or two, the urgent need was to extend the demonstration, development and training which the College could best provide.

Lessons learned from the Surf Life Saving Association of Australia

Desmond Hoare's high regard for the Surf Life Saving Association of Australia was now of special importance. He shared this regard with Kurt Hahn, who knew well the Australian President, Judge Adrian Curlewis, who has been remembered at St Donat's by the Adrian Curlewis Resource Centre in Life Saving. The Australian techniques and club organisation had demonstrated how to make life saving an exciting and challenging activity for young people. Kurt Hahn also recalled how, on a visit in 1958, Curlewis had been shocked by the headline in a British newspaper: 'THE DROWNING SEASON'. '*He made a remark which caused us to blush: "there are so few Australians – life is more precious over there."*' Desmond Hoare believed that Britain was '*light years*' behind Australia in all these matters.

In April 1966, John David, a chemist on the College staff, was awarded a Winston Churchill Travelling Fellowship to study life saving methods in Australia. He returned via the United States with the personal knowledge to become a Surf Life Saving Association Examiner and Competition Judge in Britain, and with the technical and organisational expertise to make him one of the driving forces in developing equivalent clubs in Wales. He also brought back with him an ingenious, impressively simple metal torpedo tube with a harness attached to it which he had found being used by the professional lifeguards at Huntingdon Beach in California. This torpedo tube was the lifeguards' basic piece of equipment and a great improvement on the traditional, cumbersome life saving cork ring and even the alternative flexi-tube which needs to be wrapped around the patient. It could be pushed from a short but safe distance towards a drowning albeit still conscious person. The victim could grasp it without endangering the rescuer in the water, and with it the rescuer, inside the harness, could tow the patient confidently over even a long distance. It could also be used to support an unconscious patient. In 1968 the then Director of the College's Extra-Mural Department, Chic Thompson, persuaded a businessman friend and neighbour of the College, a Mr Jones, the owner of a plastics products factory in Bridgend ('Jones the Plastics'), to mass-manufacture the tube. Its origin inaccurately credited to the College, it is now used extensively by life-saving clubs and placed by local authorities at strategic places for use by the public in emergencies. Finally, John David had returned with dramatic accounts and film of the speed and manoeuvrability of rescue launches propelled by Hamilton water jet units now being developed 'down under' for use in surf.

During filming in 1968, the volunteer girl casualty in the cliff rescue was injured by falling debris from the cliff face. This photograph recalls the sudden injection of reality that took over.

The College Extra-Mural Department

All these developments led to an application in 1966 to the Grant Foundation in New York for funds to place the extra-mural work of the College on a sounder footing. The current College Director of Activities, Chic Thompson, would change his role, becoming entirely responsible for this new department. The application listed the programmes carried out in 1964 and 1965. Courses had been offered to young people from outside the College in basic and advanced swimming, life saving, first aid, canoeing, sailing, climbing, the making of skin suits, and the handling of inshore lifeboats. They had been attended by local school children; persons sent by the Central Council of Physical Recreation; education training colleges including staff and third-year students from Loughborough; and police cadets from the Cardiff City Police, Glamorgan, and the cities of London and Manchester – in total around 800 in each of the two years.

With the success of the application to the Grant Foundation, achieved through Hahn's idealistic rhetoric and the practical implementation led by Desmond Hoare, the so-called extra-mural activities of the College gained momentum and the potential threatened soon to outrun the College's resources and facilities. Lifeguard clubs had already been established in nearby Llantwit Major and in Penybont, the latter in response to four drownings in a single season. In 1967 two additional clubs operated patrols throughout the summer on local beaches in Sully and Barry, and five rescues took place. Glamorgan, Monmouthshire and several other local councils in Wales were now providing funds. By this same year police authorities were sending instructors and cadets to the College for training from Glamorgan, the city of Cardiff, the Manchester City Police, the Oxfordshire and West Sussex constabularies, the City of London Police, Devon, Cornwall, Carmarthenshire and Cardiganshire. The Manchester Fire Service was also represented. In all, between April and September 1967, a total of 1,326 young people attended College courses and 560 life-saving qualifications were gained.

By 1968, with the Extra-Mural Department reinforced by a second grant from New York, seven local lifeguard clubs had been set up, the numbers coming to College courses had risen again, 29 lives had been saved, and there had been no fatalities on patrolled beaches. A Lifeguard Federation Committee was established under the chairmanship of the Head of the City of London Police, Sir Arthur Young, which brought together the Surf Life Saving Association, the Royal Life Saving Society, the Royal National Lifeboat Institution, the British Canoe Union and HM Coastguard.

At this time too the decision was taken to open the National Coast Rescue Training Centre at Aberavon, near Port Talbot, where exceptional facilities were already in place. For the first time, there was to be a training centre available to all the relevant life-saving organisations for training, the study of methods and techniques and the development of equipment. The warden of the Centre was to be Chic Thompson. Although Chic Thompson had not been directly involved in the College coast rescue units or played a role in the technical development of the boats, he was, as a former Commander in the Royal Navy and Director of Physical Education in the YMCA, a fine swimming coach. He also brought an unusual flair for public relations to his new task, in which he was undoubtedly strengthened by the credibility given him by the Surf Life Saving Association of Great Britain and Wales and by the record of the College. He went on to become President of the Surf Life Saving Association first of Wales, then of Great Britain, and was a key influence in promoting the birth of new lifeguard clubs and in winning the support of local councils. It is sad to record that the National Coast Rescue Training Centre was not successful in securing longer-term funding and had to close. Happily, its role has largely been taken over more recently by the RNLI with their fine Lifeboat Training Centre in Poole and their steadily growing youth and beach lifeguard schemes.

It was also now that Desmond Hoare was invited to join the Committee of Management of the RNLI, serving on this and on the Boat and the Rescue and Search Committees from 1969 until 1978.

ATLANTIC COLLEGE

(THE FIRST INTERNATIONAL ALL SIXTH FORM COLLEGE)

ST DONAT'S CASTLE
LLANTWIT MAJOR
GLAMORGAN

TELEPHONE
LLANTWIT MAJOR
HEADMASTER
DEPUTY HEADMASTER 345
DIRECTOR OF STUDIES 345
BURSAR 271
DIRECTOR OF EXTRA MURAL DEPARTMENT 597

3rd November, 1966

Dear Bill

I enclose two negatives and a print. I want five copies of a print like this to be used in a special Christmas card being designed for the College, to send to top brass in the Royal National Life-Boat Institution. We get a good deal of cash from them to keep our fleet going !

As you will see I have not been very successful in matching the two negatives. The black and white one is much too strong for the other, but I believe there is some process called reducing, which I haven't the faintest idea how to undertake. Because of this I have had to put the horizon line in the black and white level with the ship but it might be better if there were no horizon line. I wonder whether you would like to bring your technical skills to bear on this, and see what you can produce.

No hurry

yours

Desmond Hoare

D. J. HOARE
Headmaster

Dr. W. Evans,
Prior Garth,
Ewenny, Bridgend,
Glam.

Encls.

Desmond Hoare was an enthusiastic photographer. In 1966 he conspired with Dr Bill Evans of nearby Bridgend, the father of two college students and a true expert in the field, to pull the legs of the RNLI 'top brass' with a rather special Christmas card. It is reported that they were not too amused. The cartoon is one of two drawn for the well-known 'Goring' Hotel in Victoria, London.

Now tho' we thought that the wind did a little abate, yet the ship having struck upon the very dangerous sands of Nash, outside the parish of St. Donat's, we were in a dreadful condition indeed, and had nothing to do but think of saving our lives as well as we could; we had a boat at our stern just before the storm, but she was first stav'd by dashing against the ship's rudder, and in the next place she broke away; we had another boat on board but how to get her off into the sea was a very doubtful thing. God helped us for we got her off the ship and started drifting in the night. After some time we heard the crashing of the sea on the cliffs. Then the courageous rescuers found us & brought us ashore.

GEORGE ENQUIRES WHETHER THEY HAVE ANY FISH TO SELL.

CHAPTER 9

Psychedelic Surfer and the 1969 Round Britain Powerboat Race

In the early summer of 1969, in his final weeks as Headmaster before he embarked on the challenging uncertainties of developing the Atlantic College project overseas, Desmond Hoare received a telephone call from a young man, John Caulcutt, whom he rather mercilessly described as *'a long-haired young-ster who had done well on the stock market and fancied entering the Round Britain Powerboat Race in a different type of boat'*. John had no interest whatever in the construction of the boat as long as it was finished and ready to go in five weeks! By way of sponsorship £700 was available.

In mid June 1968, the owners of the *Daily Telegraph* and senior people in British Petroleum had met at the Savoy Hotel in London and agreed in principle to sponsor this race. The underlying idea was to demonstrate that Britain could produce boats capable of standing up to the extreme conditions that a circuit of Britain would entail. In the early plans, Portsmouth was to be both the start and the finishing line, and the coastal rather than offshore nature of the circuit would ensure that the general public could witness much of the action. There were to be ten stages in all, with the start on 26th July 1969 and the finish on 6th August in the middle of Cowes Week. Tellingly, the second day's run from Falmouth to

Milford Haven across the open waters of the Bristol Channel was to prove one of the most difficult and perilous.

There was much discussion, even controversy, as the entry criteria were debated and agreed. How many crew members? How much safety equipment? Was advertising permissible to help offset costs? Should there be limitations on the size of competitor craft and engine power? In the event, only the Royal Navy Brave Class Fast Patrol Boats were excluded, but a special class for vessels between 45 and 75 feet was included. By early 1969 there were 82 likely entries with another 141 expressions of interest.[9]

The organisers, the Royal Southern Yacht Club, estimated a 10% drop-out at each stage and expected only 20% of the entries to finish.

The competition boats themselves were expensive, costing anything up to £100,000. Although the cheapest, **Anglia Knight**, was only £4,000 and the majority ranged from £10,000 to £25,000 each, these figures did not reflect their real value when related to the money spent on research and development. Together with the money invested in trials, extra equipment to conform to the race rules, preparatory reconnaissance and supporting maintenance teams at each staging point ready with spares and skilled fitters, the money spent on the race was estimated at £1,000,000. A helicopter was at stand-by for the 22nd Special Air Service regimental entry, whose crew included qualified divers equipped with frogman's suits. One prominent figure in the powerboat world, Peter Thorneycroft, entered four boats of his own design and arranged for a fifth to follow him round the course with spares and workshop personnel. The Ford team set up a professional organisation with the use of helicopters and fixed-wing aircraft, their team manager plotting progress and planning tactics from the air, and the Perkins engine people likewise provided many support personnel and both a helicopter and a fixed-wing aircraft to ensure that their engines performed well.

The official safety boats were HMS **Brave Swordsman** and **Brave Borderer**, Brave Class Fast Attack craft from the Royal Navy, 98 feet long, powered by 3 × 3,500 hp diesel fuelled turbines, capable of 40 knots cruising and 52 knots maximum speed. One had to stay well clear of the transom when the turbines started up as 5-metre flames could erupt from the stern exhausts! No boats in the Round Britain Race were serious competition for the 'Braves'.

John Caulcutt – or rather Atlantic College – had a problem. It was now 20th June, and the race was to start on 26th July. No suitable boat existed, and the students were in the middle of their A-Level examinations. Desmond asked two Dutch students, Otto van Voorst tot Voorst and Willem de Vogel, and the College carpenter Roy Thomas, who had become much involved in the rescue boat workshops: *'did they think they could build a 21 foot twin-engine boat for the race in five weeks?'* Roy said no, the other two said yes. Roy's morale was subsequently

Psychedelic Surfer *at a very early stage.*

9   All the background information on the race is taken from *The Daily Telegraph – BP Round Britain Powerboat Race* by Crab Searle and the *Daily Telegraph Magazine* of Friday 25th July 1969.

Willem de Vogel and Otto van Voorst tot Voorst.

maintained by the promise of regular supplies of Dutch tobacco from Willem. *'Otto and I worked 16 to 18 hours a day. In fact, we worked so hard that we did not even take off the time to watch the first man ever to walk on the moon.'*

Otto recalls that *'they had a large degree of freedom to build a boat that they thought would be suitable for the 1700 mile race'.*

Willem remembers:

> *We had one significant problem ... we had a tube but it was not long enough. Admiral Hoare simply told me: you make it longer. This I did. It took me four days. Pumping it up for the first time was the most nerve-wracking thing I have ever done. I had night-mares that, in rough seas, my seams would not hold up. When* **Psychedelic Surfer** *completed its first day of the Round Britain race, I finally started to have faith in my tube.*

Twenty-one feet overall with a hull length of 18 feet 6 inches, it was the first boat built at the College to have twin engines which had also to be controlled by a single steering wheel. Otto wrote:

> *For the timber construction we basically doubled up on everything, more brass bolts per foot of framing and double thickness in all plywood used ... when we came to the colour scheme of the hull the choice was ours and she was painted red, yellow and black, the family colours of the de Vogels and the van Voorsts ... the mechanic on board, a RN lieutenant, insisted that the seat in the back was installed facing backwards so that the outboards could be monitored continuously. It took a long time to convince him that it*

was not going to do much good watching the twin standard 50 hp Mercs (hand start) as any potential troubles would not show up on the outside of the cowling … In the end he conceded and the three seats were all placed facing forward ….

These seats were inexpensive standard seats made for conventional trucks with normal springs entirely unsuited to a marine environment but adequate for the race.

The Surfer needed to be fitted with a radio for emergencies and sufficient battery power … to avoid the spilling of battery acid and fumes the standard screw caps were replaced with condoms which worked perfectly. When we showed this detail to DJH he was surprised at our ingenuity and asked how we had been able to find balloons to resist acid and to fit so elastically. We did not go into detail.

Willem was taken aback when John Caulcutt came to the College with one of his two crew members. It was the marine whom he had soaked so often the previous year in Plymouth Harbour.

It is intriguing to compare this building achievement with the report written by Joan Davies on behalf of the RNLI for the International Lifeboat Conference in 1976: *'Gluing the sponsons to deck and gunwale is highly specialised work, calling for controlled conditions – the air must be clean and temperature is critical. With the stretching of the sponsons to fit the hull, the preparation of wood and tube surfaces and the preparation of the adhesive solution (a very skilled job), this stage of building takes about ten days.'*

The Race Course.

The Race

Psychedelic Surfer was ready for the water after three weeks of intensive work and launched successfully in mid-July. Three weeks for the building, but not long enough for Desmond Hoare to come to terms with the chosen name or its pronunciation, which for him remained for ever *Psychede-elic Surfer*. She was trucked down to the Isle of Wight for the final preparations. The two student builders were too young to qualify as crew members but went to Plymouth and the Isle of Wight to see to the pre-race preparations and to follow the boat for the first leg of the race. On the first day, *Psychedelic Surfer* ran out of fuel going over the finishing line. According to the extensive fuel trials they had conducted, there should have been 20% left over. Willem called Desmond Hoare to report on the problem: *'Desmond never cursed in front of students.*

Psychedelic Surfer back home at the College after her triumph in the Round Britain Powerboat Race of 1969. Desmond Hoare (top left) talks with her two Dutch builders, Otto van Voorst tot Voorst and Willem de Vogel.

However, this time he did. He all of a sudden realised that we had done our fuel trials with Imperial gallons and that we had ultimately fitted out the boat with US-built fuel tanks whose capacity was expressed in US gallons. There happens to be a 20% difference.'

'We have been training for the race for weeks past and are all tremendously fit', one of the crew members told the press. 'We have a back-up team of mechanics and radio technicians and are confident that the boat will be a finisher – and well up in the prize categories.' In fact the technical back-up throughout the race was provided by Otto alone, who had to hitch a ride on another support craft each day to make it to the next port. The only problems he encountered were the need for some occasional re-gluing of tape on the outside of the tube and one delayed start when the wrong oil–petrol mixture had been put in the tanks. By happy chance the College electrician was on holiday on the Isle of Man where the problem had occurred and quickly found the answer.

At the end of the second leg in Milford Haven, a race official made this comment: '**Psychedelic Surfer** has caused astonishment by getting this far … if she hits a gale I fear she will be in dead trouble.'

The race sponsor, the *Daily Telegraph*, had this to say on 3rd August:

*the real winner – we refer to **Psychedelic Surfer** which, as each day has passed, has won a place in everybody's heart. Questions as to her welfare are as much a top priority as information on who was first, second and third on the various legs … her crew* *maintained that it is the safest boat in the race. They base this piece of wisdom on the 11 separate watertight compartments and that even if 10 should go pop, the last will keep them afloat … we not only have the smallest boat in the race, the youngest crew, and the lowest horsepower but the quickest built too.*

And on 7th August before the final leg they reported: '*these same 118 miles stand between* **Psychedelic Surfer** *and the greatest single performance of all the 24 remaining boats in this, the longest and most gruelling event in the history of powerboat racing … it is safe to say that only the crew and builders of this 23-foot rubber inflatable gave them a chance of getting round. But day after day they have emerged safely, if shaken, confident that in the end they would do it.*'

As she crossed the Caledonian Canal she had entered the newspapers as '*the new Loch Ness monster*'. With 43 starters and 24 finishers and just 12 inches over the minimum qualifying length, she came in 19th overall. No wonder at the judgement that, in terms of the cash yield against investment, **Psychedelic Surfer** did better than all her competitors! The race organisers had put her among the outsiders at 200–1. At the finishing line the crush barriers folded and the crowd surrounded the platform to give an ovation for what was the greatest performance of all the finishers. At the prize-giving too in the London Guildhall John Caulcutt received a well-deserved standing ovation.

Graham Dillon, one of the **Psychedelic Surfer** crew and an employee of BP, wrote up his experiences afterwards in the October 1969 issue of the BP house journal *Shield*:

John Caulcutt receives his prize at the Guildhall from Sir Alec Rose, who sailed round the world single-handed in 1968/9, completing his voyage a few days before his 60th birthday.

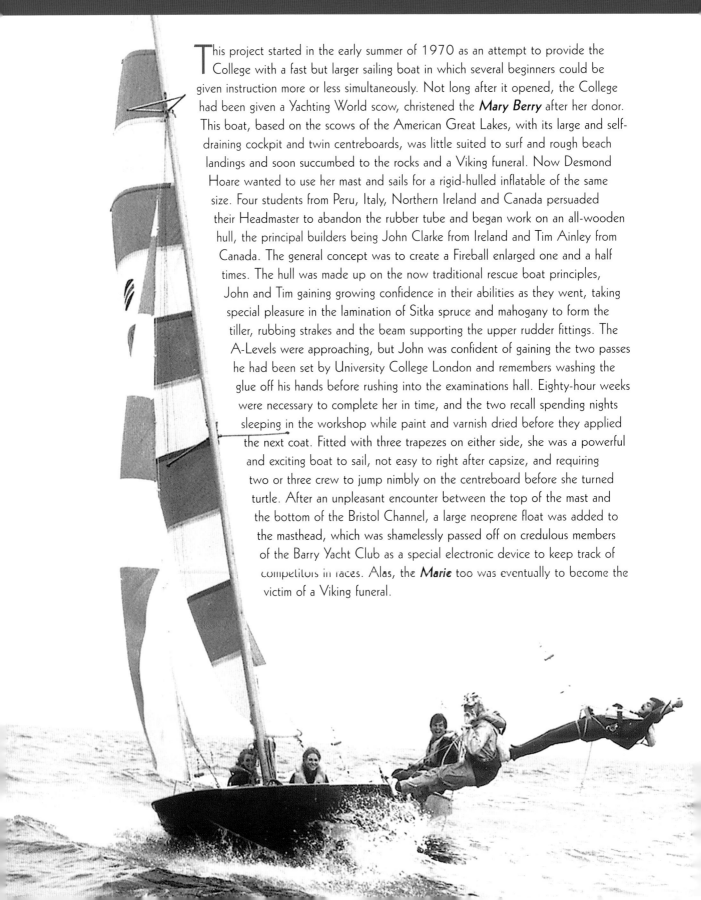

The Marie

This project started in the early summer of 1970 as an attempt to provide the College with a fast but larger sailing boat in which several beginners could be given instruction more or less simultaneously. Not long after it opened, the College had been given a Yachting World scow, christened the **Mary Berry** after her donor. This boat, based on the scows of the American Great Lakes, with its large and self-draining cockpit and twin centreboards, was little suited to surf and rough beach landings and soon succumbed to the rocks and a Viking funeral. Now Desmond Hoare wanted to use her mast and sails for a rigid-hulled inflatable of the same size. Four students from Peru, Italy, Northern Ireland and Canada persuaded their Headmaster to abandon the rubber tube and began work on an all-wooden hull, the principal builders being John Clarke from Ireland and Tim Ainley from Canada. The general concept was to create a Fireball enlarged one and a half times. The hull was made up on the now traditional rescue boat principles, John and Tim gaining growing confidence in their abilities as they went, taking special pleasure in the lamination of Sitka spruce and mahogany to form the tiller, rubbing strakes and the beam supporting the upper rudder fittings. The A-Levels were approaching, but John was confident of gaining the two passes he had been set by University College London and remembers washing the glue off his hands before rushing into the examinations hall. Eighty-hour weeks were necessary to complete her in time, and the two recall spending nights sleeping in the workshop while paint and varnish dried before they applied the next coat. Fitted with three trapezes on either side, she was a powerful and exciting boat to sail, not easy to right after capsize, and requiring two or three crew to jump nimbly on the centreboard before she turned turtle. After an unpleasant encounter between the top of the mast and the bottom of the Bristol Channel, a large neoprene float was added to the masthead, which was shamelessly passed off on credulous members of the Barry Yacht Club as a special electronic device to keep track of competitors in races. Alas, the **Marie** too was eventually to become the victim of a Viking funeral.

Before the race we wrote to 200 firms. Many were interested until they heard the boat was to be a rubber one, and then they laughed … in June, exactly one month before the race, the boat builder told us that as he was moving his factory he would not have the boat ready for another three months. The situation looked desperate. We tried all the companies who had ever made an inflatable. None of them could build one, let alone in four weeks. We then contacted Atlantic College, who said they would do it. Next day we were in Wales and finalised the design with the school's Headmaster, Admiral Desmond Hoare, and the two 18-year-old Dutch students who were to build the boat, Willem de Vogel and Otto Van Voorst … now a dream looked reality – in 25 days we had a sophisticated inflatable power-boat, 20 feet 9 inches long, powered by two standard 50 hp Mercury outboard motors …

On the Friday before the race … we took the boat to Souters Yard, but they refused to scrutineer the boat, saying it was not suitable for the race. Eventually we persuaded the scrutineers that we were serious, so they let us through – after six and a half hours …

… by this time people, especially the competitors and race officials, no longer laughed at us but were trying in every way to help us. They cheered whenever we made another stage in the race, and articles began to appear about us in the press.

Since Milford Haven, Otto Van Voorst had been with us every night to help with repairs on the boat, and he was to prove invaluable. Otto travelled in style on HMS Brave Swordsman which also carried our suitcases …

Progress was good though and we averaged twenty knots. Three boats were forced to retire that day (Inverness–Dundee) and many others damaged their propellers and rudders on sandbanks …

The leg from Dundee to Whitby … was our roughest one yet. Force five winds over the shallow coastline, especially the Firth of Tay, pushed up some very big seas and progress was accordingly very slow … none … thought that Psychedelic Surfer could have survived those seas, but once again we proved them wrong … it took us just over ten very wet hours to make Whitby, but when we got there we had our biggest welcome yet. The crowd of 3,000 on the quay started cheering, and the other competitors who were in before us started up on their sirens. It was then that we learned that one boat had sunk, and a large number of others had had to retire – we were very lucky …

All went well until fifteen minutes from the finish, when we cut the corner at Selsey Bill to dodge the tide race and found ourselves in shallow, rocky water, surrounded by lobster pots. Twice we stopped with pot markers round the propellers, but these we managed to clear and to a tumultuous welcome we crossed the line off Southsea. We were brought ashore on the beach, and faced a barrage of press and TV cameras and a flow of champagne! The only boats to get this welcome were the first two boats and ourselves. It was a great honour and a fabulous end to the race.

Desmond Hoare knew that this could be the great opportunity and breakthrough. He arranged for RNLI crews all round Britain to be alerted to **Psychedelic Surfer**. It was the defining moment in the entry of the rigid-hulled inflatable into the British and the international rescue and powerboat scene.

CHAPTER 10

Yet more X Boats and the Final Outcome – the RNLI B-Class Atlantic Lifeboat

In addition to the drama of **Psychedelic Surfer** in 1969, these were busy years at the College of very active boat building and the consolidation of ideas and practices.

From X9 onwards most of the RNLI testing was carried out at the College itself by visiting inspectors. There can be no doubt that the regular visits of these inspectors to St Donat's were both inspiring and mutually enjoyable occasions even if, early on, one of the student helmsmen had managed to shipwreck his inspector crew on Nash Point quite literally by cutting corners (the inspector was not too impressed). It was also clear that the RNLI personnel were excited by the enthusiasm of the students. It was, after all, in many respects a new world for them, and the international mix made it all the more intriguing.

Lieutenant Commander Ted Over had been in charge of both offshore and inshore lifeboats from 1969 until 1972 before being transferred to Head Office. It was he who was initially entrusted with the introduction of two RNLI proto-types on the lines of the Atlantic College boat, one a 14-foot C-Class version with a single engine, the other a 21-foot craft with twin engines. At the time the Royal Navy was also seeking the next generation of ships' boats. A demonstration was

Later X boats

X9, begun in March 1969, was an enlarged version of Xs 7 and 8, once again with a tube specially produced by Avon but fitted with a bigger engine, a Mercury 65. She was a powerful and highly reliable sea boat, capable of 30 knots and fitted with lights for night operation. The flat underwater area was carried right forwards to the bow, as also applied shortly thereafter on **Psychedelic Surfer**. The resulting strength of her hull was well proven one afternoon when her coxswain allowed her to be caught on incoming surf. She overshot the trolley and continued most of the way up the concrete slip on her own. She was back in the water the next day. She remained in service for many years but had no new design features beyond the additional equipment for night work.

X10 was the glass-fibre boat already mentioned. Not used as a call-out boat at St Donat's, she had her moment of glory nonetheless in North Wales in the summer of 1970. Two students had taken her there on holiday and had invited out the helmsman of the Pwllheli Inshore Lifeboat, Mr R. W. Vowell. He was already, in the words of the Station Honorary Secretary, 'extremely interested in this craft and had "swallowed" her hook, line and sinker', when they came across the disabled yacht **Teetana** and towed her to safety.

The X11, 19 feet in overall length, was a slightly refined version of X9, spacious and extremely well balanced, fast, strong, economical on fuel and, in the opinion of many, the most successful of them all. The principal student builder was again a Finn. Immensely strong and a fine sea boat, with a flat underwater shape rising to the bow, she too survived the Bristol Channel for many years.

X12, 16 feet 9 inches in overall length, was built for twin engines which were supplied by the RNLI to test the night operations potential of a smaller hull. She tended to throw her bow up into the air, a defect that was only partially cured by the fitting of wedges underwater at the stern.

arranged in Old Portsmouth, with the RNLI invited to display a rigid-hulled inflatable. A committee of senior captains and a group of interested parties from the Ministry of Defence, Bath and naval establishments was assembled to watch a 'steam past'. The 14-foot prototype, with RNLI Deputy Superintendent and Engineer Mike Brinton at the helm and Ted Over as his crew, approached the viewing platform at 25+ knots, making a sharp turn at the last moment and deluging the assembled spectators with spray, after which the crew resolved to return without further delay or ado to their base at Cowes – all of which only proves that the RNLI personnel were not above acquiring bad habits from College students, who were very practised in this technique when wishing to irritate their friends aboard Fireball dinghies.

But it was now that the RNLI took the design into a new era with, as Ted Over expressed it, some 'dead donkeys' on the way. His successor, David Stogdon, taking over from him in 1972, was able to focus the full RNLI resources on the Atlantic 21 development. There could not have been a better, more admirably qualified person, especially in personal terms.

David's father and grandfather had both been housemasters at the public school Harrow. A schoolboy accident had prevented him from taking his School Certificate, so he completed his education by setting off to Czechoslovakia to learn German. He was already an adventurer. As a small boy, just 7 years old, he had persuaded his mother to buy him a small rowing boat from the pond at Frinton-on-Sea which he then rowed out into the North Sea until he could just see the church spire on the Essex coast. As a teenager he had sailed a 12-foot dinghy from Fowey to Falmouth (and been towed back home when the wind fell). He joined the RNVR in 1938, and it was claimed that he was able subsequently to enter any harbour in Britain without charts. He was the gunnery officer on HMS **Tynedale**, which had forced a U-Boat to dive shortly before the ill-fated attack on

After the hull has been formed and planked upside down, it is placed upright on the jig to have the floor added. This photograph illustrates clearly the six watertight compartments that eventually form the hard hull (in addition to at least five equally watertight compartments in the tube) and the strong stub transom that holds the outboard engine without impeding in any way the exit of water taken aboard.

St Nazaire, thus helping to maintain surprise. A year later HMS **Tynedale**, was sunk in the Mediterranean by the same U-Boat captain. David's idealism and diplomacy subsequently made it possible to bring this captain to a St Nazaire reunion of survivors in the 1990s.

After the war, David joined the RNLI and had been their Chief Inspector in Scotland in the fateful year of 1953 when two lifeboats were lost with only one survivor in each crew. He visited their families, then set himself the task of trying to ensure that there would be no more lifeboat widows. His son Matthew lived his life in the same spirit, having been engaged in charitable work in Botswana, Borneo, Papua New Guinea, Indonesia, Qatar and Iraq before losing his life driving in a convoy for the United Nations High Commission for Refugees in Croatia during the break-up of Yugoslavia.

David Stogdon had become interested in the rigid-hulled inflatable idea around the same time as the College and had built an early prototype at the RNLI base in Borehamwood. However, he quickly recognised that the College was on a more promising path and, after completing his own two designs for the Royal Navy, had been a regular visitor to St Donat's and an enthusiast for the ideas evolving there. Once he had become the Superintendent of the RNLI base at Cowes, assisted by his Deputy Mike Brinton and the Deputy Chief Inspector Tony Wicksteed, he promoted the clear distinction that was now emerging between offshore and inshore operations and the craft needed for these different tasks.

Xs 9 to 12 were all test driven by Stogdon and other RNLI inspectors. An old problem remained controversial and unresolved – the underwater shape, especially towards the bow. A narrowing but flat run up towards the bow gave a stronger hull overall and an easier 'fit' onto the beach trolley but harder pounding upwind and against the waves. The College helmsmen had become adept at turning their boats at an angle to the wave at the last moment as they reached the crest, thereby sharply reducing the pounding effect, but this nimble manoeuvre carried the serious risk of engine cavitation as the propeller left solid water. The consequences were erosion of the propeller blades caused by the small, exploding air bubbles as the hull jumped out of the water, and the high risk of a suddenly racing engine leading to a fractured and lethally dangerous flywheel. The evidence was always visible on the propellers at the end of each sea-going session – the black paint was stripped away around the stem – and, until they were rumbled at it, members of the beach recovery teams who handled the trolleys would duck quietly out of sight and give the incriminating propeller some rapid treatment with a spray can.

Numerous experiments with the positioning of spray rails did not solve the fundamental problem, and handling the boats at speed in a following sea also continued to depend on rapid student reaction. This was highlighted in dramatic fashion one winter afternoon when David Stogdon, crewed by College students, took the otherwise admirable X11 into the Nash tidal race and drove her at top speed 'downhill'. In these conditions the College helmsmen knew their boats and always eased off on the throttle as they reached the trough, but David wanted the truth. He found it. X11 hit the bottom of the next wave at full speed and might as well have been driven into a brick wall. One girl crew was catapulted over the bow and was indeed fortunate that the boat was no longer moving. Happily, she was made of stern stuff, was planning a career in the Merchant Navy, and was the Penny Sutton who, as already noted, became the first fully registered female crew member to take part in an RNLI inshore call-out service in 1972.

David Stogdon thought X11 *'was marvellous, like a big toboggan, but not for us'*. College experimentation continued.

X13 was given a miss – seamen are superstitious. In fact, **Psychedelic Surfer** was the thirteenth X boat.

In 1969 X14 was commissioned at RNLI request as *'an utterly basic boat for unsophisticated crew'* with a 40 hp Evinrude tiller-controlled engine and with a new tapered tube now being promoted by its maker, the Avon Rubber Company. Avon were also building and marketing their new sports boat, and the RNLI wished to evaluate the one against the other and with other boats available on the commercial market. X14 was purchased from the College by the RNLI and led directly to the creation of the C-Class inflatable lifeboat.

The Adventures of *Jemima Puddleduck*

X15 was built for College use with wheel and remote throttle control and, very experimentally, a Hamilton jet unit attached to the 40 hp outboard in replacement of the conventional lower unit and propeller. Smaller than her predecessors, narrower and with a larger length–breadth ratio, she had a shallow V hull and was intended for life saving off a surf beach. Impressively, this small boat could also out-perform a larger IRB with greater horse power like X11 when tied stern to stern with both boats powering away from each other. The water jet unit also came in handy for soaking other crews and fellow students with its water discharge. Perhaps this was the reason she was named **Jemima Puddleduck**. In the end, the high revs and the consequent cracked flywheels and scored piston rings led to the substitution of a standard mercury outboard of 40 hp. For flag-flying reasons **Jemima Puddleduck** was taken to the river Thames, where one of her student builders had a summer job. Despite strict instructions on the need for observing the prescribed hours of running-in for a new engine, her two student builders, being 18-year-olds, took the approach of an irate-looking swan as a justifiable reason for getting her onto the plane, thereby completing the journey between two locks in 20 minutes fewer than the time imposed by the 4-knot speed limit and earning themselves a well-deserved and severe reprimand from the irate lock keeper.

Not long after, **Jemima Puddleduck** was loaded onto a 48-foot powerboat and taken to Cowes, where the powerboat owner, a marine salesman, indulged in non-stop alcohol-fuelled partying. On the third day this boat and her euphoric crew had disappeared and were pursued out to sea and overtaken halfway across the Channel by **Jemima** and her Atlantic College student crew, who explained their pursuit by maintaining that they had been concerned about the capabilities of her skipper and his five crewmates. In fact the skipper was thoroughly drunk, there were no charts on board, the compass had not been swung, the planned destination of Alderney can be testing under any circumstances, and the fuel tanks were nearly empty. The engines eventually spluttered and died in the dusk several miles short of the French coast, the boat was taken in tow by **Jemima**, and the voyage was completed in darkness as the student skipper followed a succession of fishing boats into harbour. Without papers, none in the crew could go ashore; without going ashore they could not refuel. Eventually the French authorities relented, and the return to Cowes was made with a chart supplied by a British neighbour in the roadstead. The two **Jemima Puddleduck** students arrived back at the College two days late and the Admiral, now no longer the Headmaster, having heard the full story, covered up for them. The new Headmaster (and author) first heard the facts nearly 40 years later.

The Final Step

X16 was similar to X15 but had a less eventful career and was distinguished principally by having been entrusted entirely to a female crew. She and her predecessor had been built at an RNLI chief inspector's request for a twin-engined boat that was strong, seaworthy and easy to handle, suitable for night operation but light enough for beach launch, and capable of 30+ knots.

X17 was commissioned by the RNLI as one of three final prototypes for the eventual B-Class Atlantic lifeboat, the other two being built on the same principles but with modified underwater lines in Cowes. David Stogdon had a hand in her design. An error in the construction of the building cradle led to a greater curve in her hull than in her two partners, and she became known to some as the 'banana boat'. Fitted with twin 50 hp outboards, she was driven by Prince Charles on a visit to the College on a cold and windy day in November 1970. Later, equipped with more powerful engines and under the name *Fundracer*, she took part in the Cowes–Torquay–Cowes powerboat race, failing however to finish in severe conditions. At the time she was nonetheless the largest, fastest

Teamwork between the boat and trolley crews was always a vital part of successful and safe sea-going.

HRH Prince Charles, later President of the UWC International Council in succession to Lord Mountbatten, goes to sea in X17, one of the last prototypes before the realisation of the first RNLI B-Class Atlantic Inshore Lifeboat.

rigid-hulled inflatable afloat. With one more change in the bow design because of the continuing suck-down problem, this prototype effectively became the RNLI's Atlantic 21 B-Class lifeboat. The first of these was placed on service in 1972 in Hartlepool on the east coast. In reality they were the direct descendants of **Psychedelic Surfer**. As Desmond Hoare noted, this was the end of the Atlantic College development story. There had however been some subsidiary developments before reaching this point, just as there were innumerable refinements carried through subsequently by others, but the fundamental concept was in place and proven.

The RIB moves abroad – Singapore and Canada

Now, as was natural and proper, the RNLI effectively took over the innovative work with their professional, full-time staff and carefully targeted funding. Desmond Hoare was spending increasing amounts of his time abroad on ambitious development of the United World Colleges project. The Bristol Challenge had meanwhile been the birthplace for a magnificent response from which life-saving societies were to benefit the world over. So it was a matter for relaxed amusement and chuckles that X18 should become known as 'double trouble'. She had two tubes, one mounted on the other, the lower fitted to a small mini-boat-style hull. The intention was again to investigate a boat that was lighter and more easily handled by a small beach crew. The tubes experienced difficulties in remaining attached to one another and the boat as a whole enjoyed parting company with the water. So she is best forgotten. X19 was not a success either, student interest having now been allowed to focus rather too enthusiastically on speed and the adoption of contemporary high performance powerboat design. She had a tendency to shed crew members overboard in tight turns. For safety reasons she was taken out of service and accompanied Desmond and Naomi Hoare into retirement in Southern Ireland where, with more modest engine power, she finished her days as a platform for mackerel fishing.

X20 was built by former Atlantic College students in Singapore, working under Desmond Hoare's remote control and to now well-proven plans, for the second United World College that was emerging there. February 1972 saw Desmond Hoare writing to his friend Tom Norreys of the Avon Rubber Company:

> *You may be amused to see the enclosed photograph and to know that the first of your large tubes is now flashing around in Singapore. The second will be built shortly. This one is named* **Harapan Antarabansga** *which means 'International Hope' ... the Canadian College is due to open next year. I think there will be a couple of former students over on the site on Vancouver Island making the first safety craft which will be to the same design.*

Vancouver Island was to be the home of the third United World College, which opened in September 1974.

X21, built at Atlantic College in a combination of thin marine ply and internally laid GRP, was a 13-foot ultra-light boat, with convex hull and deck sections.

The first rigid-hulled inflatable ever in Singapore!

The idea was to exploit the material properties of this composite structure, putting the ply under compression. She had only one central, longitudinal fin but a series of transverse stringers to create the form. The complex construction was completed by student enthusiasts over the Christmas break between 1971 and 1972. There are no reliable surviving reports of her performance.

The second Singaporean boat was X22, and two further boats, 21 feet in length and to virtually the same design, were constructed, again largely by former Atlantic College students, for the Canadian College. It was becoming difficult to imagine new colleges coming into existence without them. Although the term X (experimental) was now redundant, and indeed with Desmond Hoare's accelerating withdrawal from the scene no longer legitimate since they expressed so vividly his personal imprint, the two Canadian craft had new constructional features. The first was of thin plywood construction with internal hand-laid GRP. The hull again had the traditional five longitudinal fins but was injected and packed with closed foam. She was completed in 1974 and engined with twin 85 hp Mercury outboards. Her successor was constructed in GRP, a mould having been taken from the first. The hull was once again filled with closed cell foam. She was fitted with an inboard–outboard petrol engine and completed in 1975.

In reflecting at this time on the experience gained, Desmond Hoare retained his scepticism over deep V hulls, which were such a problem to handle on trolleys. He acknowledged that the enthusiasts for speed would prefer the V hulls until the day when they were succeeded by

The Bristol Channel in peaceful mood.

aerofoils, and hydrofoils and hovercraft, all basically unseaworthy in small size … this new sort of activity is outside our present competence to experiment … the safest type of power for close inshore rescue work may prove to be the water jet, well demonstrated in Australia off surf beaches … development here to RNLI requirements has yet to start … perhaps hardly worth the money except for launch off sand beaches but we just don't know!

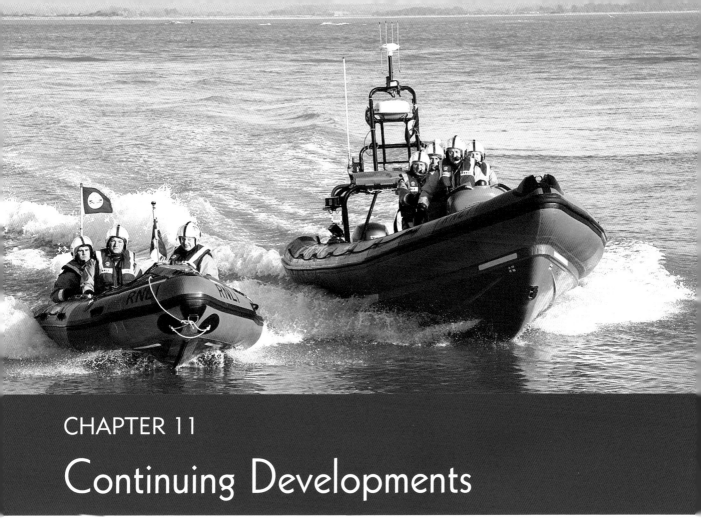

CHAPTER 11
Continuing Developments

David Stogdon recalled taking an Atlantic 21 to an International Lifeboat Conference in the United States in 1971 and, in the sea-going demonstration, having to run down a long swell by tacking. The combination of the fine bow and blunt stern was continuing to make these boats difficult to handle in a following sea. As reported by Joan Davies to the Lifeboat Conference in 1976, a revision of the bow lines was proposed by Ray Chatfield of William Osborne of Littlehampton and trials were carried out together with the Wolfson Marine Craft Institute of the University of Southampton. The new bow was deeper, with a finer entry, and the deck was raised in the forward section to maintain comparable buoyancy. The difficulties of building this finer bow in ply led to the adoption of glass fibre. All later boats had this redesigned bow entry. They were the Atlantic 21 Mark 2, numbered by the RNLI from B 508 onwards. Desmond Hoare's design was used for about seven boats before this modification came in. All the early RNLI boats up to B 540 were built by William Osborne at Littlehampton. From B 542 onwards the construction was taken over by Halmatics. All the RNLI boats were also soon equipped with twin engines.

Inevitably and rightly, there were many other modifications and improvements. The most important was no doubt much encouraged by the consequences of the RNLI's readiness to show off the Atlantic 21 to fellow lifeboat societies. The Dutch were especially interested and were invited to test an Atlantic 21 off Hurst Castle in the Solent. This was early on and, by good fortune, a second hull had been completed by the RNLI and was in attendance. The Dutch Chief Inspector Bernard de Jong, accompanied by Alan Reynolds of the Wolfson Unit and Mike Brinton from the RNLI, took over one of the two boats. After running for a while with and against the seas, Alan Reynolds decided to run parallel with a breaking wave and flipped over. There followed a long and wet journey home with an upside-down lifeboat in tow. It was not long before the RNLI had developed a roll bar across the transom with a buoyancy bag which could be inflated with a gas cylinder, enabling the boat to be righted within about 18 seconds. There were also the necessarily sophisticated arrangements for water-proofing the engines and enabling them to re-start immediately after immersion. This bar was a useful location for navigation lights, for radio equipment, for the protection of crew should capsize occur in very shallow water, and as a handhold for crew moving aft to the engines. A series of alterations was also made in the helmsman's Delta console, enabling the other two crew members to be more securely seated and to have better all-round visibility. The flexible fuel tanks were replaced by stainless steel tanks which could be cross-connected in an emergency, and which were henceforward incorporated in the hull. Experimentation was also carried out with water ballast tanks, the idea being to enable the intake of water near the bow to keep the bow of the boat down when breaking out through heavy surf.

Desmond Hoare and Bob Hale at work on the four-seater canoe intended to achieve perpetual motion on the green waves rolling up the Bristol Channel.

Cost and speed of repair and replacement must be major priorities for the RNLI and by 1976 the first Atlantic Class Mark 3 was under construction. These considerations dictated many of the most radical changes. One in particular would have given satisfaction to all those students with broken hacksaw blades, sore hands and glued-up fingers: the gunwales were now being moulded with a concave curve at the outer edge to house the tube which, in one unfruitful experiment, was attached to the hull by luff ropes drawn through grooves on each side of this curved section. The deck was made in two parts and bolted to the hull, with all the increasingly complex electrical and other equipment being very carefully housed for both security and accessibility. The savings in maintenance time and costs become impressively clear when one reads of the procedures when a boat came in for maintenance:

> the outboard engines can be unshipped and taken to the machine shop; the sponson slipped off and taken to the tube workshop; the deck, complete with all electrical equipment and engine systems unbolted and removed to clean-area benches, and the hull wheeled into the main boat shed. All parts can be worked on in parallel in the most suitable surroundings. Equally, if either sponson or hull is damaged, its replacement will only mean about a day's work … for fleet operation, the intention is to achieve an interchangeability of units, thus reducing the necessity to withdraw boats from service for other than major repairs …[10]

RNLI Newquay, Atlantic 85 inshore lifeboat, The Gladys Mildred.

By 1991 the B-Class Atlantic 21 had given a remarkable performance: service launches 15,601, lives saved 4,717, assistance to a further 2,802 persons. There were 49 on station with another 26 available for relief. In all, 95 had been built. But the greater weight of equipment aboard was leading to reduced performance, and a survey was commissioned to find a replacement. This led to the Atlantic 75.

10 *Development of the Atlantic 21* by Joan Davies for Lifeboat International, 1976.

By comparison with the 21, the length of the Atlantic 75 was increased by 12 inches (to 7.5 metres, hence the name), the beam by 2 feet 2 inches, and the bow redesigned to give a finer entry, the flat section being reduced from 22 inches to 14 inches and the finer entry extending further aft. Wind tunnel tests were carried out up to 60 mph, and she was designed for launch and recovery from slipway, davit or open beach. The six longitudinal compartments remained; a forward crash bulkhead was added, and the instrumentation was improved and re-positioned to give better visibility. With twin 75 hp engines, inversion-proofed as had already been achieved with the 21, she had fuel capacity for three hours on full throttle at 34 knots and could carry up to 22 survivors together with the crew of 3, making 9–12 knots with this maximum load. But the Atlantic 21 left very warm memories: *'The Atlantic 21 has been such an exciting efficient boat and its correctness for purpose is smack on target'*, in the words of Alan Tate, the then Superintendent of the RNLI Inshore Lifeboat Centre.

But of course progress did not stop there, not least in the light of all the developments emerging in other organisations abroad, and in 1998 the RNLI commissioned the Fast Inshore Boat 1 project as part of a wider review. The stated operational requirement was for a twin-engined boat capable of more than 35 knots in Force 7 conditions, a crew of 3–4 and a righting capability after capsize. Invitations to 21 manufacturers led to the receipt of 14 design proposals and three short-listed boats being tested over a three-day period of structured trials. The unanimous conclusion at the end of this rigorous process was that the Atlantic 75 was the best option for further development. The outcome was the new 8.5-metre Atlantic 85, with a four-man crew, twin 115 hp 4-stroke engines, a roll-bar righting system which achieves recovery from the capsized position in 22 seconds, a variable water-ballast system which enables the helmsman in 45 seconds to load 220 litres of water in the bow section – the better to break through surf – and to jettison this extra weight in 2 minutes, the hull being of a carbon/foam structure. The console was improved with the instrumentation enabling the helmsman to concentrate on handling the boat with only heading and depth displayed to him directly, the radar plotter being handled by other crew.

Beyond the RNLI

The worldwide growth in the use of rigid-hulled inflatables has been dramatic.

After a series of tests, the British Royal Navy adopted the boat with enthusiasm and by 1981 had some 70 in service, all new construction ships being equipped with diesel-driven rigid-hulled inflatables. These came to replace entirely the traditional whaler sea boat for rapid rescue and such tasks as transferring mail, stores and personnel between ship and shore or between ships. These requirements also brought a new challenge – that of launching and recovering the boat from the mother ship while under way. A Royal Navy speaker at the Conference of the Royal Institution of Naval Architects in 1981, which had been convened to review the status and record of the rigid-hulled inflatable, reported that *'the performance of all RIBs on the water is greatly superior to that of existing Whale and Gemini inflatables. RIBs can be launched and operated in Force 6 conditions and have on occasions experienced Force 8. Boat crews vie with each other to drive the RIB.'* He added that experience had shown that the risk of capsize at sea was negligible and that self-righting gear could be dispensed with for naval boats.

At roughly the same time the US Navy, its interest sparked by a report from the US Coastguard, had also become interested. The Coastguard had stated that *'in recent years a relatively new type of craft has developed in England primarily as a shore-based rescue boat. The evolution of this craft to shipboard launch and retrieval by the British Royal Navy and its seeming success has whetted the curiosity of those highly involved in such operation.'* In 1982 the US Navy acquired a 24-foot rigid-hulled inflatable from Avon/Galt to determine its potential as a ship's boat. Until that time their life-saving and rescue boats had been 26-foot motor whaleboats. In trials the rigid-hulled inflatable was launched and recovered at speeds up to 12 knots using a single point davit.

It was however the North Sea oil industry that rapidly became the critical investor and the stimulus to the most radical and challenging adaptations of the original concept and in the most severe and challenging environment. And with good reason! When Occidental Petroleum's oil platform **Piper Alpha** incurred a gas leak, caught fire and exploded on 6th July 1988, 167 men lost their lives.

An ARRC bare hull at the factory. The concave shape of the upper edge takes the inflatable tube sponson. (See Appendix 3 p. 140).

A British Petroleum ARRC (Autonomous Rescue and Recovery Craft) at slow speed. The sealed superstructure provides a righting movement in the event of capsize. See Appendix 3, The British Petroleum Story, by David Nockels on page 140.

Nearby support ships launched rescue craft in an attempt to rescue those who had jumped into the sea. The only ones able to go right inside the jacket structure were two Atlantic 21s. One was caught in the main explosion 22 minutes after the initial outbreak of fire when the entire platform blew up and her crew perished. The other saved several men and was able to get out in time. Her coxswain was later awarded the George Medal. No other rescue craft had been able to follow them. In total there were only 61 survivors.

A speaker at the same conference of naval architects was able to pinpoint the reasons:

The old tradition ... that a man overboard was a dead man, has died along with too many of the men ... attitudes have changed ... oil men, for example, are on the whole not sailors but drillers, mechanics, welders, electricians and engineers. The mystique of the sea does not attract them, they want to be safe and to live ... we live in an era of instant information … due to the dramatic nature of the endeavour, news of any casualty assumes immense proportions and public opinion demands that safety be a major consideration for big oil companies.

All these events led the oil companies to become acutely safety conscious. The risk of a man-overboard situation on offshore platforms and offshore work vessels had always been considered high. By the mid-1970s the RIB had already been identified as the ideal rescue craft – easy to launch, quick to reach the casualty and quick to return to the safety of the platform. They were launched by crane or special davit and recovered in the same manner. Nowadays all offshore platforms, drilling rigs, work vessels, standby vessels and supply boats are equipped with RIBs, which have become highly sophisticated craft with inboard diesel engines, water jet drive, full night capabilities, and radio and radar, and can be launched and recovered from heights of 30 to 40 metres.

Perhaps the leading influence in pressing forward with extreme innovation and testing in the 1970s was the Robert Gordon Institute of Technology, based in Aberdeen and operating out of its Offshore Survival Centre in Stonehaven. The Institute had already made clear its judgement that there was a need to improve the methods of rescue and standards of rescue craft used by offshore operators in the continental shelf area, and that the package must include parent vessels, fast rescue craft and the means of launch and recovery. It commissioned two larger boats, the OMR 24 and the OMR 36, both designed and built by William Osborne of Littlehampton, the aim being to achieve a higher degree of comfort for both crew and casualties and to improve yet further the sea-keeping qualities.[11] The use of a watertight cabin served both to improve the installation of navigational and other equipment and to provide the self-righting leverage in the event of capsize. Halmatics also built larger boats for the North Sea, their 22-, 24-, 28- and 30-foot craft undergoing evaluation and entering service in 1975–6. The preoccupation with capsize is interesting in the light of the comment from W. Leech, representing the Colne Group at the 1981 conference: '*As the largest operator of rigid inflatables in the North Sea with craft launched in all weathers up to a wind speed of 45 knots, operating reports from Masters indicate that even a near capsize has yet to be experienced …*' A major problem, first tackled by the Royal Navy, was that of launch and recovery at sea from larger vessels, also in heavy weather, for no davits had yet been designed for rigid inflatables. Allied with this dilemma was the absolute need to ensure that engines could be started immediately and without fail every time. Despite its very high power-to-weight ratio, the outboard engine was proving no longer acceptable because of its need for meticulous maintenance and the dangers of fire that accompanied the use of petrol.

11 But was it true, as rumoured, that the leader of this research had difficulties recruiting crew after once surfing over the lock gates into Stonehaven Harbour in the OMR 24 when he discovered that they had been closed because of very heavy weather?

ARRC

A closer view of an ARRC showing the casualty recovery area with its removable section of tube sponson and the special deck profile.

There were other developments too that showed how far matters had progressed since those pioneering days only ten years earlier on the Bristol Channel. In Canada, for example, Hurricane Rescue Craft were working on behalf of Gulf Oil to ensure that rigid-hulled inflatables could continue to operate in temperatures as low as –40 Celsius. Shaun White, the Managing Director of Ocean Dynamics Ltd, described how, to enable their Atlantic Eagle boats, weighing 2.5 tons and jet powered, to break through extreme surf, it was necessary to inject one third of the boat's weight into a specially designed bow section in the form of water: *'Once through the surf, the water must be evacuated immediately ... the Castoldi 06 water jet will suck this out in under one minute.'* And, in another indication of the severe conditions for which the rigid-hulled inflatables were now being designed and built, it was suggested that everything must be done to avoid capsize, and that, by filling the hull with water, the craft would drift like an old-fashioned life raft *'hanging awash supported by its inflatable collar ... this complete flooding can be accomplished in stages depending on the degree of danger'.*

And there were somewhat fantastic echoes too at the conference of Naomi Hoare's missed encounter with James Bond in one presentation. The *'fully submersible RIB'* shall be

> *conventional but with the ability to be sunk in shallow water up to about 50' ... for covert military operation on hostile shores ... able to be called up from the sea bed for instant action, having laid dormant perhaps for many months ... sunk by its crew, dropped by parachute, or from a mother ship or even by submarine ... deployment*

manually or automatically by coded radio signals to a small aerial floating on the
surface or by acoustic signal … or by satellite relayed signals from afar …

Two conclusions drawn by the Robert Gordon Institute were nonetheless a comforting, indeed flattering, endorsement of Desmond Hoare's ideas:

The single most important factor in maintaining control and stability of a craft after
a washout is a speedy clearance of water shipped … and … it is fundamental to the
design of a rigid hulled inflatable that the hull is a fair compromise between as soft a
ride as possible into a head sea and a good ride in a following sea both when travelling
faster or slower than the sea … The propulsion system must allow rapid acceleration
so as to overcome certain sea states …

Also of great formal significance was the 1983 Amendment to the International Conference for the Safety of Life at Sea of 1974, adopted by more than a hundred maritime nations in Regulation 47, which stated that '*Rescue Boats may be either of rigid or inflated construction or a combination of both*'. This decision led Stanley Williams, a marine consultant and Librarian of the Royal Institution of Naval Architects, to comment:

The significance of these events should be recognised as marking the true coming of
age of Hoare's child and the work of adoptive parents during the formative years …
If it had not been for the pioneers the new regulations on rescue boats [in Chapter III
of SOLAS 74] could never have been written. In fact it is they who wrote the speci-
fications over the last twenty years. We owe a debt to all of them and to Hoare who
started it all.

The Mini-X Boats

Some years before the finalisation of the designs and experimentation that led to the B-Class Atlantic 21 Lifeboat, there was a related line of development that failed to achieve its full potential. This was the mini-boat.

Drowning can happen very quickly indeed and Desmond Hoare had recognised the need, especially on large and popular beaches manned by professional lifeguards, for a small fast boat that could be launched instantly and operated in very shallow water by one person. The College accordingly built a series of MX rigid-hulled inflatable boats which were fitted with 10- and 18-hp outboards and had lengths ranging from 10 feet 6 inches to 12 feet 6 inches. The original prototype, MX1, 10 feet 6 inches long, was capable of 17.5 knots with a 10 hp engine and 22 knots with the 18 hp engine. It could even manage 19 knots with two aboard and 16.5 knots with three, thereby demonstrating its ability to return swiftly to shore with casualties. It required extremely careful handling. One uncomfortable memory of College sea-going was the time when an inexperienced helmsman, alone on board, was thrown into the sea by his own sudden change of direction on the tiller helm and was then circled several times by his own boat, still under power, until another boat was able to intervene and rescue him. Boats with the more powerful engines undoubtedly required remote wheel steering and throttle control. The then Chairman of the RNLI Boat Committee drove a mini-boat at St

Three examples of mini-boats: tiller driven, wheel steering, and, in the beach shot, *Jemima Puddleduck* fitted with an experimental water propulsion unit attached to a standard outboard engine. Her ability to operate at speed in very shallow water was impressive.

Donat's but decided that there was no RNLI requirement for such a craft and it accordingly had a lower priority in the College programme. It had nonetheless a remarkable rough-water performance for so small a boat, with the extra power of the larger engine being important when breaking through surf. The prototype was used for a summer season at Dawlish in Devon, where it successfully handled a number of incidents.

One of the College mini-boats was also equipped with an outboard with a water propulsion attachment. It performed impressively in very shallow water. At this time, as noted, the Australians were already experimenting with extremely fast hard-hulled craft off surf beaches. Not only could they operate in very shallow depths, they were also safer for bathers and others in the water because they did not have the lethal propellers which can be such a peril with normal propulsion. Their two drawbacks were their considerable weight and their clumsy handling when going astern. The College mini-boat engine suffered severe cavitation problems with its water jet unit, with the consequent danger of a fragmenting flywheel owing to sudden and excessive revolutions. But this was an opportunity lost, an opening for beach rescue work that would have deserved longer-term exploitation.

In all, the College built some ten mini-X boats, several of them being sold off to beach rescue units around the country.

CHAPTER 12
The Dutch Experience

The Winter Issue 1981/2 of the RNLI journal *The Lifeboat* had suggested that the Atlantic 21 was the Institution's most efficient and cost-effective craft. She had also attracted worldwide attention from other lifeboat societies. Foremost among them was the Dutch Life Saving Society, the Koninklijke Nederlandse Redding Maatschappij (KNRM).[12]

David Stogdon was by now the RNLI 'face' of the rigid-hulled inflatable and a sought-after lecturer:

> *Once when I was giving a talk to the IMCO,[13] the Russians switched off the lights in the hall, walked past my table in the dark, and when the lights came on again all my Atlantic papers had gone … they use RIBs now with their factory ships. Boats not exactly to our designs are to be found in Australia, Canada, USA and Russia …*

12 The KNRM was created by the 1991 merger of the two previous societies, the Koninklijke Noord en Zuid Hollandse Reddings Maatschappij (KNZHRM) and the Koninklijke Zuid Hollandsche Maatschappij tot Redding van Schipbreukelingen (KZHMRS).
13 Inter-Governmental Maritime Consultative Organization, re-named the International Maritime Organization in 1982.

In the late 1970s he had persuaded the RNLI to build on this success and had begun the development of the Medina Class Lifeboat. The prototype was shown at the London Boat Show in 1979: 39 foot overall in length, she was intended to cover the operational gap between inshore and offshore rescue. Equipped with twin diesels, she had a sharply veed bow for an easier passage upwind with 9 feet of 29-inch flat surface on the rear section to enable her to remain upright when beached. This configuration, with the tubes clear of the water unless heavily loaded, also assisted planing at speed. The first model was named **Mountbatten of Burma**, another coincidental link with the Atlantic College since Mountbatten had been the International President of the United World Colleges from 1967 to 1978, and the original local appeal for funds for her development had been launched one week before his death at the hands of terrorists in Ireland. With hindsight regarded as a mistake, the design was abandoned – chiefly, it seems, because no satisfactory solution was found for her propulsion.

The Annie Poulisse *being launched off the beach at Zandvoort.*

Just one week into retirement in 1981, David Stogdon was invited to become a consultant to the Dutch KZHMRS. At the 21st International Lifeboat Conference in New York in 1970 the Chairman of the Royal South Holland Lifeboat Institution had requested the RNLI to supply them with an Atlantic 21 together with some preliminary training. They had gone on to acquire two further Atlantic 21s in 1975 and 1979. Whilst the RNLI retained the view that these remained inshore boats, David Stogdon now encouraged the Dutch to go for bigger craft. They

The most recent of the Arie Visser class, the Antoinette, *built in 2009.*

The Dutch Atlantic 75, the Dolfijn.

were the more free to do so, being able through Stogdon to learn from the Medina programme without having either involvement in its disappointing history or financial losses arising from it. Indeed the Northern Dutch Society now joined forces with the South in funding this new development. The KZHMRS built its first rigid-hulled inflatable in 1983–4 at the IJmuiden yard of Mulder and Rijke, naming her the **Koningin Beatrix**. The 'KB' was eventually sold in 2008 but is still in operation as a ferry to windmill farms on the Dutch continental shelf. In her 24 years of working life as a rescue boat she was strengthened a few times and re-engined from Perkins to Volvo. She provided the Dutch Life Saving Societies with an enormous amount of experience and information.

In 1984 the Northern Society (KNZHRM) commissioned the naval architect Willem de Vries Lentsch, in consultation with David Stogdon and Professor Gerritsma of the Technical University of Delft, to design the first 'northern' RIB. She was launched in 1987 and named the **Johannes Frederik**, the first of the JF-class lifeboats, of which six altogether have been built.

The JF lifeboats were an outstanding learning project. From 1990 they were placed alongside the traditional boats in Force 7 upwards and were found to be their equal or better. They had a rather flat forward section to avoid burying the bow in following seas. Once they were found to be safe in these conditions, attention was turned to reducing the slamming upwind. The V section was redesigned to a steeper form with the bow itself extended and given the same rigid volume as before, the tube tapering from 80 to 68 cm at the extreme bow. The hulls were strengthened three times with more frames, thicker hull plating, stronger girders and improved fastening of the superstructure to the deck. Sister ships already in operation had to undergo the same costly upgrading. These boats were originally equipped with fine Deutz air-cooled engines, but the environment of salt water and salt spray, combined with big cooling air inlets and exhausts, wreaked havoc in the electrical part of the engine room, and the change was made to MAN water-cooled engines. The larger size also made possible the consolidation of the concept of the superstructure, essentially the deckhouse, providing the necessary buoyancy to effect recovery following capsize, an option clearly not available in the smaller open boats.

In 1993 the JF boat *Jan van Engelenburg* was on call-out off Terschelling in a strong Force 10 gale, with an average wave height of 8 metres and extremes of up to 12, the roughest conditions, according to the Dutch Meteorological Institute, for 20 years. A traditional lifeboat launched on the same operation was hit by a heavy ground sea which deformed the side window and damaged the video plotter, mast and chart table. By now, both boats were inside the ground sea area along with the casualty, a German cargo vessel, which was clearly destined to run ashore. The *Jan van Engelenburg* decided to head back out to sea but was then caught by a side wave and leaned over some 160 degrees. The crew now fastened their safety belts and proceeded seawards, to be capsized bow over stern. Recovering quickly to the upright position, they found damage only to the flying bridge windscreen and the radio antennae. The engines were restarted and operations resumed. The key lesson was that, in extreme conditions, seaworthiness is not enough and capsize safety is more important. A subsidiary lesson, solemnly noted, was the need to fasten down the ashtrays!

All three Dutch developments of the RIB conducting a large-scale emergency evacuation exercise off a ferry near the island of Texel.

The knowledge gained with the JF boats, the continuing involvement of David Stogdon, and the professionalism of the building yards Aluboot (Hindeloopen) and Habbeke (Volendam) led directly to the rapid and successful design and introduction into service of the smaller *Valentijn* (1988) and the larger *Arie Visser* (1997) type lifeboats.

By 2009 the Dutch had built the following:

Class	Dimensions	Engines	Prop	Speed
Arie Visser (AV) 10 boats	19 × 6.8 × 1 M	MAN 2 × 1000 Hp	Water jet Hamilton	35 knots
Johannes Frederik (JF) 6 boats	15.4 × 5.4 × 0.8 M	MAN 2 × 680 Hp	Water jet Hamilton	33 knots
Valentijn 16 boats	11 × 4.1 × 0.6 M	Volvo 2 × 450 Hp	Water jet Hamilton	33 knots

The Dutch invested boldly in water jet propulsion for all their larger craft. While requiring a little more maintenance than propellers, these units make the boats extremely manoeuvrable, they are more efficient at high speeds, and they meet the demands for handling breaking seas and towing broken-down craft admirably. The problem of operating them in thick ice or in water fouled by oil was solved by the introduction of a pipe that is pushed down through the hull to a depth below the ice and oil pollution, enforcing a reduction in speed to around 10 knots, regarded however as entirely acceptable in such exceptional circumstances. Their boats rapidly proved themselves able to survive the worst sea conditions, including heavy breaking seas over offshore sandbanks, and by 2001 the Dutch had replaced all their earlier boats with rigid-hulled inflatables.

They were equally innovative in the use of new constructional methods and materials. Their tubes, for example, are made of two layers – the outer layer the coated fabric hypalon, the inner layer neoprene. Between the two layers there is 1-inch foam. Thus in the event of damage to the outer skin there is still an inflated

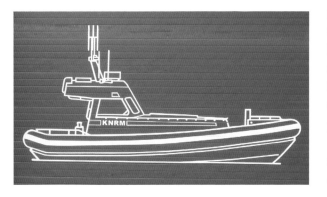

tube. The capacity of the tubes to absorb the energies of the sea is a key contributor in Dutch eyes to the seaworthiness of all, and especially the larger, lifeboats. The all-volunteer crews have great confidence in their craft, not least because all the larger lifeboats are reliably self-righting, a quality they have demonstrated on several occasions in 25 years of operation.

The two societies, following their amalgamation in 1991, now operate a total of 70 vessels at 42 stations, some equipped with reserve craft, ranging from 4 to 19 metres in length, of which 15 are of the Atlantic 21 or 75 class. Their Arie Visser class is three times the size of the early RNLI inshore lifeboats, with a top speed of 35 knots and a carrying capacity for 120 survivors. Their Valentijn class, an 8.3-ton craft first stationed at Noordwijk aan Zee in 1991, is equipped with modern hydrostatic drive and can be launched off the beach by a trolley that is operated by a single person.

The Dutch experience has demonstrated utterly convincingly the impressive ability of these fast craft to handle very large waves and breaking seas, likewise the effectiveness of powerful water-jet propulsion.

One of these Valentijn craft was 'repatriated' into Britain in 2004 and is now in service at the independent lifeguard station of Caister on the Norfolk coast. Some experts consider the Dutch to have the finest and safest fleet of rescue boats in the world.

Some 50–75 rigid-hulled inflatables are also operated in The Netherlands, in close cooperation with the KNRM, by the autonomous Reddingbrigade, especially during the summer, on the beaches and in the lakes, canals and rivers.

The College generously acknowledged

The RNLI, despite the Dutch experience, remains of the view that the far longer and more varied British coastline requires a more flexible approach, and continues to invest in a variety of craft to suit the contrasting local conditions. Ironically, the Maritime Rescue Unit, formerly the Robert Gordon Institute of Technology in Aberdeen, discovered an abandoned Medina hull in Liverpool, originally built in 1984, stripped, lengthened and modernised her, fitted her with Hamilton water-jet propulsion units and operated her very successfully from their base at Stonehaven near Aberdeen.

The Valentijn-class Paul Johannes, *launched at Noordwijk in 2007.*

Ray Chatfield, who played the key role in the redesign of the Atlantic 21 bow section, once said: *'I will never forget David Stogdon of the RNLI predicting to us in 1974 that this type of craft would eventually be used worldwide'.*

In letters in December 1993 about the Dutch developments, David was generous in acknowledging the College's role: *'Atlantic College started something which will affect all lifeboat societies in time ... there was a wonderful spirit at the College and everyone wanted to have a go at designing a boat. It was largely this spirit which helped us develop the inshore lifeboats round the British Isles.'* It is true that he had other memories as well. *'I remember being horrified by some of the shapes being attempted by the boys and girls and being told by the Admiral: "Don't worry, we are all going to learn a lot from it." One rather short and round boat looked like a tea tray with a tube on it. Admiral Hoare said "try this one but be careful". It went well forward but when you turned a corner it continued just as fast sideways on the original course.* Later he wrote:

> *All their [Dutch] boats will be designed to your principles ... the large boats are 15–16 metres and the small beach boats 10 metres ...all their lifeboats will be in the 35–40 knot bracket ... the slowest acceptable speed for life-saving will be 25 knots soon in Europe ... the Italian Coastguards have built 24 of the Dutch 10 metre boats which are all based on the Atlantic College design through Desmond and then through me ... these large boats have great power for safety and over 7–10 years in service in all weathers ... full speed has been maintained nearly 90% of the time at sea ... the rigid hulled inflatables are so much better and safer than the conventional lifeboat...*

Prince Bernhard of The Netherlands visiting the College on 26th September 1966 and being shown the boats by the Dutch student and boat captain John van Kuffeler.

This all seems a fitting sequel to the visit of Prince Bernhard of The Netherlands to the College on 26th September 1966, but there is another connection as well. The van Lynden family forms part of the Dutch nobility and was granted its title in 1815 when the Kingdom of The Netherlands was founded. The Friesian branch of the family has died out, and their estate is now a school for underprivileged children. Their last representatives, Baron van Lynden and his daughter Comelia, in addition to donating the estate to the School, made major gifts to a hospital in The Hague and to the KNRM, the Dutch RNLI. This support paid for a 10-metre rowing and sailing lifeboat, built of mahogany and launched in 1897 and named the **R. Baron van Lynden**. She remained in active service until 1927 in Ouddorp and for a further year in Hoek van Holland. A second rescue boat, also named **Baron van Lynden**, was launched in 2008. It is an Atlantic 75. It has been funded by moneys from the original gift that for years had been devoted to supporting the widows and children of lifeboat men lost at sea, a rare need now taken over by the state. The van Lynden family has been well represented at the College.

CHAPTER 13
Update on the Atlantic College and the United World Colleges

In the summer of 1969 Desmond Hoare, at his own suggestion, had given up the headship of the Atlantic College to devote himself to overseas development. We had, after seven years, still only one College. This had to change.

The Atlantic College maintained its rescue commitments, albeit without the impetus of a continuing developmental role in equipment, training methods or extra-mural work. The Bristol Channel remained the Bristol Channel. In May 1969 the delay in raising the alarm cost the life of a boy who, reports suggest, was seen alive in the sea. In June four persons cut off below the cliffs by the tide were successfully assisted out by a swimmer on a line to the College boat that had been anchored beyond the area of ground swell. In July an unsuccessful search was carried out for a missing boy whose body was found by police the next morning; he had fallen over the cliffs. In May 1970 the College crews reached a distraught father cradling his small son in his arms only 3 metres from the water's edge – this boy too had gone over the cliff. In August the boats were called too late to save a young girl missing in the sea off Porthcawl; the crew included Kristin Hostvedt, the younger sister of Elisabeth, on her second service, although she was not yet officially registered with the RNLI. The following April another boy fell, from

Recovery after a night operation.

cliffs between Southerndown and Ogmore, fracturing his skull. Already in the hands of a doctor, the patient was transported with the doctor by the College boats to a waiting ambulance on Southerndown beach, the greater speed and ease of transport by comparison with a long stumble over difficult rocks probably contributing to the boy's eventual recovery. An adult man was even more fortunate, surviving a cliff fall in July 1971 and being landed safely by the crews at the College slipway; he was suffering from concussion, a broken hip, a broken arm and damage to his leg.

In July 1973 the College had its first true night service. The boats were launched at 23.40 in response to red flares at sea. Nothing was found and the boats returned to the slipway at 03.00. It was realised that searchlight equipment would have been invaluable. One interesting discovery was that the crew aboard the official RNLI Atlantic B Call boat, wearing identical clothing (skin suits and oilskin jackets) to the crew of the College boat X11, were very cold, whereas the X11 crew had remained dry and warm. The RNLI boat with its V-shaped bow had been constantly swept by incoming spray; X11 with its flat surface running up to the bow had remained dry.

In September 1973 the first service 'manned' entirely by female crew occurred. A rubber dinghy had capsized west of the College slipway. One of three fishermen, without a lifejacket, who had become separated from the dinghy, was picked up first. A second fisherman, in the water and holding on to the dinghy, was picked up next. A line was then attached to the upturned dinghy, which was towed out to sea clear of breaking surf with the third fisherman lying across the upturned boat.

This was a high quality performance, carried out under difficult conditions. All three victims required treatment for exposure.

Not all operations, it is true, were quite so serious.

On 26th May 1983, B 530 launched following a request from Coastguard Swansea. The first four crew members to arrive at the boathouse were, as it happened, all on the distaff side: Dickey Brader from The Netherlands, Christine Hage from Denmark, Philippa Cooke from the UK and Christine Lundqvist from Sweden. After engine failure and six miles of drifting in the middle of the Bristol Channel, those rescued had only one comment: '*If this is the type of crew you guys send out, you may well see us stranded off here again. We thought Christmas had come early.*' On 3rd July 1985 the boat was launched at Swansea's request to investigate a report of 20 animals sighted afloat (more or less) off Ogmore. '*Some sheep wreck*' ran the subsequent report! When a group of 7, including an elderly lady and two toddlers, were rescued and brought back to the station after being trapped beyond Nash Point by the rising tide, the leader expressed some surprise, saying he had thought that '*high tide was next week*'. A swimmer reported by a passing dredger in the sea off East Nash Buoy turned out to be a young German tourist who thought that the buoy was the limit of the safe swimming area.

Nor were the injuries always quite as serious as reported at the time. On 6th October 1977 the College Cliff Rescue Unit had assisted two Cardiff University climbers in difficulties on the cliffs between Ogmore and Southerndown. One had, according to the Coastguard Report, '*sustained injuries of broken ribs and a broken arm after falling 15 feet. There was a hole in the back of his helmet caused by a finger of rock which had not touched his head. There was no doubt that wearing a helmet had saved his life.*' College students met this same person exactly ten days later climbing at Three Cliffs Bay on the Gower Peninsula. '*He expressed thanks to us.*' And one has to admire, or perhaps envy, the amorous couple who flatly refused rescue despite two further hours on their precarious perch before the tide receded!

The Cliff Rescue Unit, a call-out unit, was always called upon whenever the casualty was on or below the cliffs. The Beach Rescue Unit was on the other hand concerned with patrol and prevention in the summer months and had responsibility for Southerndown Beach in June, July, August and September. It also took a full part in all events of the Surf Life Saving Association, competing for the first time in the National Championships in 1964 and winning them against adult competition in 1968 and 1970. The team withdrew in 1969 on an issue of principle when in the lead after the qualifying events: at the last minute and contrary to earlier firm assurances, an all-white team from South Africa was allowed to participate in the finals.

The extraordinary emphasis placed on the rescue services at the Atlantic College initially created problems for those who were keen to see this founding College joined by others. How could additional colleges be set up unless they too had the same kind of active commitment to first aid and life saving in a

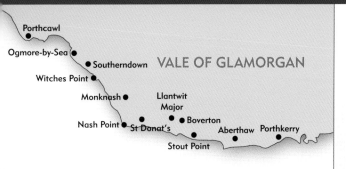

FEBRUARY 1974: The body of a police inspector, who had entered the sea off Porthcawl in his underclothes in a partially successful rescue attempt, is brought ashore in an exposure bag.

MAY 1974: A 15-year-old boy survives a 30-metre (100-foot) fall into the sea near Southerndown and scrambles ashore at the base of the cliffs. From there he is brought out to the rescue boat by crew members who swim in to assist him and is returned safely to the College slipway, wrapped in an exposure bag.

MAY 1974: Another young boy, badly injured and unconscious after falling 50 metres (150 feet) over the cliff edge near Boverton, is placed on a stretcher, the rescue boat having been beached in calm conditions. The casualty is then transferred by boat to Summerhouse Point where he is transferred into a waiting ambulance. This incident demonstrates the value of the re-design of the console and deck arrangements, making possible the carrying of a full-sized stretcher. Carrying the casualty over a long distance across the rocky foreshore would have greatly reduced the boy's chances of survival.

FEBRUARY 1975: Two fishermen are swept off the rocks at Ogmore by heavy surf. Both are recovered by police who enter the water. One policeman, however, is dragged out to sea by the undertow and is recovered in an exhausted state by the College boat.

JUNE 1975: A broken-down speedboat with three adults and two children aboard is recovered safely.

JULY 1975: Recovery of a body from Stout Point to the slipway, believed murdered.

AUGUST 1975: Recovery of a body from the sea one mile west of Monknash Combe. The casualty had rescued two bathers six days earlier but had himself been swept out to sea.

FEBRUARY 1976: Four boys are recovered safely from a stranded position one mile west of Llantwit Major.

JULY 1976: A young boy is recovered dead after a fall over the cliff at Dunraven and is brought back to the College slipway to lessen distress to his parents waiting on the nearby Southerndown Beach.

AUGUST 1976: A car goes over the cliff at Nash Point. The elderly driver had experienced trouble in engaging reverse gear. Two bodies are recovered by the College Cliff Rescue Unit and brought to the College slipway.

MAY 1977: A boy falls over the cliff into the sea at Southerndown and is transferred to an ambulance on the beach. He recovers in hospital.

MAY 1977: A man goes over the cliff near Southerndown and survives because the tide is high. He is brought out from the base of the cliff to the rescue boat by a swimmer on a line and landed safely.

OCTOBER 1977: An injured climber is carried by members of the College Beach and Rescue Units to an ambulance waiting at Southerndown Beach.

MAY 1978: A married couple and their dog are recovered safely from below the cliffs at Nash Point and landed at the College slipway.

MAY 1978: A 10-year-old child falls over the cliff a mile from Llantwit Major while bird nesting. His father, unaware of what has happened, arrives on the beach minutes before the child's body reaches the ambulance but is hustled away into a car by the police in an effort to mitigate his distress.

AUGUST 1978: A cliff fatality at Southerndown. A photographer falls, his equipment lying smashed all around him.

AUGUST 1978: A boy over the cliff east of Llantwit Major is recovered dead by stretcher by the College Beach Rescue Unit.

APRIL 1979: A motor cruiser in difficulties off Nash Point with two adults and two children aboard is recovered safely on the College slipway.

APRIL 1979: Of two climbers between Southerndown and Ogmore, one falls and injures his ankle; the other is stuck on the cliff face. The first is lowered into the College lifeboat and landed at Southerndown Beach; the second is raised to safety by the College Cliff Rescue Unit.

MAY 1979: A female suicide victim is recovered from the sea east of Llantwit Major.

AUGUST 1979: A long search with refuelling in mid-operation is carried out for a missing 8-year-old boy at Ogmore in cooperation with a helicopter and the Porthcawl inshore lifeboat. The College Beach and Cliff Rescue Units are also involved. The boy's body is washed ashore three days later.

SEPTEMBER 1979: Two casualties are landed at the College slipway from a broken-down motor vessel 1.5 miles SE of Nash Point.

AUGUST 1980: Four persons are landed from a broken-down motor boat off Aberthaw.

AUGUST 1980: While the College boat is on night exercise to the west, it is called by the police to the recovery, possible only from the sea, of two men who have fallen, apparently drunk, over 30 metres (100 feet) from cliffs at a caravan site near Aberthaw. Refuelling at sea off St Donat's, the boat proceeds to the accident site and recovers the two bodies, handing them over to the police in Barry Harbour.

OCTOBER 1980: An unsuccessful search for a body reported floating in the sea off Dunraven. A car is found at the foot of the Southerndown cliffs, reportedly a suicide of a family of three. One body is recovered two days later.

MAY 1981: A car is found at the top of the cliff at Dunraven with a suicide note. A body is found below and transferred by the College boat to Southerndown Beach.

MAY 1981: A body is reported off Witches Point. The boat is launched in a strong swell off the slipway and the body is found 300 metres offshore, face down and in heavy clothing. A swimmer enters the water. One tube is partially deflated to facilitate the recovery aboard of the waterlogged body. The casualty is found still to be breathing and is given resuscitation. He is lifted four minutes later by helicopter but does not survive. Four College students (Michael Barker from Britain, Lars Linstedt from Sweden, Adrian Lunn from the Bahamas and A. Mohammed from Pakistan) receive Letters of Commendation from the RNLI for this service.

JULY 1981: The College boat recovers two boys from rocks to the west of Southerndown. Two more are raised to the cliff top by HM Coastguard. Yet two more are rescued from the rocks at Nash Point by the College boat on its return to the slipway.

JULY 1981: Two adults are recovered by the College boat from a stranded position 460 metres (500 yards) east of Nash Point; five others are brought to the cliff top by the College Cliff Rescue Unit; two further persons are discovered stranded on the way home but decline assistance.

MAY 1982: An unsuccessful search for a swimmer washed off a dinghy off Southerndown Beach., The body is later recovered by helicopter.

AUGUST 1982: An unsuccessful search for a fisherman washed off the rocks at Witches Point.

JULY 1983: An unsuccessful search for a man reported in the sea off Aberthaw who is later washed ashore, an apparent suicide.

MARCH 1985: A boat is reported abandoned off Aberthaw with five persons missing. All are recovered in a joint operation with Barry lifeboat and helicopter but all perish.

SEPTEMBER 1984: The College boat stands by as the body of a drunk is recovered from the base of the cliffs at Southerndown.

OCTOBER 1988: A body is recovered from Porthkerry Beach.

MAY 1990: An exhausted and cold surf ski paddler is recovered from west of Nash.

DECEMBER 1990: A body is recovered from between the College and Llantwit and is returned to the College slipway.

MARCH 1993: The recovery of a body from Temple Bay.

JUNE 1993: Four persons are reported overboard from a small motor pleasure boat, one swimming ashore to raise the alarm.

Two are recovered by College boats and given resuscitation; one is winched up by helicopter. All recover later in hospital. For this service the College crew (John Barr, maths teacher and houseparent from Britain, Annie Berube from Canada, Jane Heaton from Britain and Lorenz Breitfeld from Germany) receive Letters of Commendation with a special emphasis on the quality of the first aid rendered.

MARCH 1994: An unsuccessful search for a person drowned following a fall from the cliffs. The search is repeated twice the following day. The body is finally recovered later in the same month.

MAY 1995: A body is recovered from the sea.

JUNE 1995: An injured person is brought to the College slipway.

JUNE 1995: Three swimmers swept offshore are recovered from the sea.

JUNE 1996: Two persons cut off by the tide are brought in safely.

JUNE 1996: Another two persons are recovered safely after being cut off.

APRIL 1997: One person is recovered safely after injury following a fall from the cliffs.

JUNE 1997: Three lives are saved of persons cut off and in danger of being swept away by the tide.

JANUARY 2001: The police are assisted in the recovery of a body from nearby Boverton Beach.

JULY 2002. A pleasure boat with two aboard is brought to safety.

AUGUST 2002: A boat with four aboard is towed to safety.

JULY 2003: Two children and one adult are recovered safely from the base of nearby cliffs.

AUGUST 2005: A body is landed. No explanation for the tragedy is available.

JULY 2006: Two are rescued from the cliff base under Nash Point and brought out to the boat on the swimmer's line.

AUGUST 2006: Two teenagers are recovered by boat from the base of the Dunraven cliffs.

SEPTEMBER 2006: The recovery of a body.

JANUARY 2008: A body is recovered from the sea and landed at the slipway following a long search involving several different rescue units.

MAY 2008: Two persons are recovered from the cliff base at Witches Point.

AUGUST 2009: Unsuccessful search for a boy reported swept off Porthcawl Pier.

The Crown Prince and Princess of Japan visit the College in the summer of 1976.

really rigorous natural environment? The height of absurdity appeared to have been reached when a proposal for a College in a gentle wine-growing region in Germany suggested that it could qualify for United World College membership by having students on stand-by for drowning emergencies in the Rhine some 15 miles distant, this idea being the follow-up to a truly vigorous and serious debate about the comparative value of sea and mountain for these matters. Nonetheless, the Singapore International School had joined the UWC in gentle stages, first becoming an associate school in 1970 before moving on to full membership. The Lester Pearson United World College of the Pacific opened in 1974 as a memorial to the great Canadian statesman and Nobel Peace Prize winner. Others followed until, in 2009, there were colleges in Swaziland, Italy, the United States, Hong Kong, India, Norway, Venezuela, Costa Rica and Bosnia, with a 13th college opened in Maastricht in September 2009 in partnership with the Dutch Ministry of Education.

The Atlantic College has continued to evolve. The adoption of the as yet largely untested International Baccalaureate in 1971 for all students new that year gave it a national role in the proving and publicising of this adventurous, pioneering development in international education. The NATO image of the early days was already fading in the 1960s but received its death blows with the arrival in 1974 of the first Chinese students to attend a secondary school outside communist China – all 12 stepping out of the bus wearing Mao suits and clutching the all-important little Red Book. Then came the enrolment of the first student from the Soviet Union, accompanied by an extremely competent Russian teacher of physics.

These new arrivals did much to dispel stereotypes. No one was more excited to meet Lord Mountbatten, relative of the tsars, than this Russian physicist who, whilst at the College, designed and built an innovative small windmill with adjustable vanes for greater efficiency – he later gained a British patent for his invention. Wishing to demonstrate this machine to the visiting Lord Mountbatten by powering up a light bulb in a worryingly feeble breeze, he equipped a student hidden in the cellar below with a push bike for standby emergency current. Nor could one fail to be impressed by the subsequent careers of four of that first 'Mao' generation: the Foreign Office diplomat, the high-ranking military officer, the female Secretary of the Chinese Movement for Nuclear Disarmament and the young man called to the capital Beijing to manage its future tourist trade (he was sadly killed shortly afterwards in a road accident) – all of them engaging during the visit of the new College Headmaster to China in vigorous discussion as to which one of them was making the greater contribution to peace.

There was also continuing maritime adventure. The College joined forces in 1971 with the National Trust for Scotland, the Nature Conservancy, the Army and the Brathay Hall Exploration Group to undertake vegetation mapping, some highly focused ornithology and a sheep census on St Kilda and the neighbouring

Two College boats off the islands of St Kilda.

islands off the west coast of Scotland. The Animal Breeding Research Station at Roslin, near Edinburgh, was also anxious to find out how the sheep on Boreray had survived and adapted since they were abandoned in 1930. Two College boats were transported north and carried out to the islands by landing craft of the Royal Corps of Transport. Transferring crew and supplies on to the island of Dun with a swell rising and falling 3–4 metres (11 feet) was exciting. The puffins could be heard muttering in their underground burrows, of which it was estimated that there were some 50,000. The sheep on Boreray had developed the interesting habit of charging straight at humans rather than running away from them but, with the aid of ropes on the steep and slippery slopes leading down to the rocks, seven specimens were eventually 'swum out' to the boats by students in their skin suits.

Desmond Hoare's final contribution

Desmond Hoare had one more contribution to make to Atlantic College seafaring.

Coming to grips in his Provost role with the combined needs for more money, more publicity and a wider 'world' view, he dreamed up the idea of a world voyage under sail with rotating crews composed of former students. These students, meeting across their College generations, would relive some of their formative experiences in Wales, renew their enthusiasms, and give their time and money to act as lively ambassadors with important audiences around the globe on behalf of the expanding United World Colleges. It would all take two years and lacked

Sea Star off the College before beginning her round-the-world voyage.

Sea Star being seen off from Tower Bridge on the Thames by the Prime Minister Edward Heath, the President of the UWC International Council Lord Mountbatten, and Patron of the Voyage Thor Heyerdahl, just visible on the right of the picture.

nothing in ambition. His first letter to the Dulverton Trust in September 1971 suggested an initial fundraising target of £250,000 and even that the whole venture might become a permanent feature of the organisation. '*In the long run*', he wrote later, '*this [UWC] project should be largely directed by former students and if they see it as I do, as open-ended, new Colleges will still be being created at the turn of the century and until every country in the world has one or more of its own.*'

After a careful search the vessel was identified – **Sea Star of the Hebrides**, a 96-ton Sparkman & Stephens centreboard ketch, built in 1959 with 3,500 square feet of sail and a length overall of 90 feet with a 22-foot beam. David Wills of the Dulverton family and a Deputy President of the UWC Council decided to purchase the yacht himself, making her available to the voyage organisers on extended loan. The skipper too was found – Peter Williams, an experienced sailor and coach of the Royal Yachting Association and, most importantly, the father of a College student. His wife Maywen came too as purser, cook, nurse and crew 'mother'.

The departure lacked nothing in ambition or publicity. The joint voyage patrons were Maryon Pearson, the widow of Lester Pearson, and Thor Heyerdahl. The crew were seen off from London Bridge on the Thames on 25th June 1973 by Lord Mountbatten, the International President of the United World Colleges, and the Rt Hon. Edward Heath, the Prime Minister. **Sea Star** then set off across the Atlantic, calling over the next few months in Montreal, Toronto, where the astronaut John Glenn came aboard, Halifax, Boston and New York, where they were given the Freedom of the City, Chesapeake Bay, Washington DC, Annapolis, Miami, Nassau, Puerto Rico, Panama, Hawaii, Yokohama, Hiroshima, Nagasaki,

115

Hong Kong and Singapore, where she arrived in July 1974. The return trip to the UK went around the Cape of Good Hope as the Suez Canal was still closed. But, as Desmond was fond of reminding his students, the great thing about the sea is that it always brings you back to square one. The voyage was a magnificent experience for the scores of former students who took part. It was the accountants who were left at square one.

As **Sea Star** was returning home, another more modest but satisfying marine venture was taking shape. A champion crew from the Freshwater Bay Surf Life Saving Club in Sydney was touring Britain in 1975. Excited by the international nature of St Donat's, they left their boat behind for the College. Slow, heavy, but dramatic in action and requiring the utmost in discipline, teamwork, stamina and cool-headedness in big waves, the Australian surf boat was a real challenge. Five students from Germany, Norway, Poland, Sweden and Zaïre trained for nine months in 1975 with sufficient determination and skill to become the British national surf boat champions. Beforehand, their historian coach John Hemery, emulating John David, had won a Winston Churchill Travelling Fellowship, again to bring himself and the College up to date on life saving in Australia and New Zealand. Funds were raised; QANTAS, the Queensland and Northern Territories Airline System, donated free flights; and the surf boat crew flew out to Australia with him for a short season of competition in December and January of 1974–5 as guests of the Surf Life Saving Association of Australia. They took part in races and events up and down the coast of New South Wales, achieving huge publicity for the United World Colleges and enjoying unforgettable hospitality.

The College surf boat crew of 1974–5 in training.

CHAPTER 14
X23 and Marine Science

In 1972, not long after the introduction of the International Baccalaureate, a small staff team, led by the later College Principal Colin Jenkins, took advantage of IB regulations to work up and introduce a new course in marine science. At the same time the College also brought in sub-aqua diving as an additional activity.

Before long, and thanks to his daughter who taught English for a while at the College, the biologists were in touch with Professor R. S. Glover, the Founding Director of the Institute of Marine Environmental Research in Plymouth. Professor Glover visited the College. The immediate outcome was extensive use of College students in data collection for environmental survey analyses of the Bristol Channel, mostly under the leadership of the College's Dr James Mendelssohn. Academically able and highly motivated students who could go to sea in almost all weathers throughout the year were an unusual resource for a research department. Members of the Plymouth Institute also did some studies on stress levels in mussels, using the College as the base for their work.

A major survey was commissioned around this time into the ecological implications of building a Severn barrage. The Barrage Investigating Committee was chaired by the Scientific Advisor to the government, Sir Hermann Bondi, who was already a Visiting Fellow of the College and later to become a member of the Governing Council. It was decided to construct a General Ecosystem Model for the Bristol Channel and the Severn Estuary (GEMBASE). From this model it appeared that the animal life in the Bristol Channel needed more food than was provided by the phytoplankton. One answer could have been that seaweed was responsible for making up the deficit. However, the current estimates militated against this explanation, and the College was entrusted with the conduct of a comprehensive survey of seaweed levels throughout the Channel to provide a hard number for the model. This daunting task lasted almost day in, day out for over a year and was led principally by Dr Arthur Gaines who, after a spell on the College staff, went on to the Marine Biological Institute in Woods Hole, Massachusetts. The GEMBASE investigation required the division of the coastal areas of the Channel into 1 km squares, representative squares being selected for analysis. The seaweed was collected along carefully laid transects at 10-metre intervals from the high water mark down to the lowest underwater depth at which it continued to exist before the lack of light prevented growth. Low tide was chosen whenever possible to make the task easier. The weed was collected with an ingenious three-sided quadrat equipped with a net into which the weed floated upwards after having been cut from its base, to be dried, weighed and finely cut in the College laboratories. Samples of this dried material were then taken to Plymouth where they could be burned and the ash weight measured by teams working there. As it turned out, and rather as expected, seaweed was not the answer, and the extra food must have come in from the land around the Channel as, for example, autumn leaves and sewage. However, no organisation other than

*X23, the **Lundy Puffer**, begins to take shape.*

The size of X23 meant that moving her at the various stages of her construction required many hands.

the College could have collected all this material, given the requirements of time and expertise and the constraints on funding.

The College students, the skin suits, the boats, the sub-aqua diving programme, the academic course in marine science and the link with the Research Institute in Plymouth also led directly to another major enterprise – a role in the setting up of Britain's first underwater national park around Lundy in collaboration with the Lundy Field Society.

Lunde-oy: Norse for Puffin Island! Eleven miles from the mainland and twenty-two miles from her supply port Ilfracombe, her steep cliffs continue to descend 40 metres (130 feet) below the waves. They were once part of a 150-metre (500-foot) high granite and slate tor or high cliff, standing in the valley of the river Severn. The island is a giant breakwater against the Atlantic gales. Henry III built the still-standing chapel in the 13th century, and the inhabitants remained loyal to Charles I long after mainland royalists had given up the King's cause. Largely abandoned by her inhabitants in the 20th century, Lundy has 280 recorded bird species of which 35, including puffins and the rare Manx shearwater, are once again breeding on the island after the eradication of invasive rats.

But how to get there independently? The answer was X23, the largest boat built at the College and Desmond Hoare's final design. She was not finished before he retired to Ireland, and her completion was only achieved thanks to the unrelenting determination of an American student, Bruce Cowger, whose truly impressive dedication to getting her into the water drew practically the entire College to her early-morning launch on a suitable high tide in the spring of 1974.

The triumphant early-morning launch of X23, her principal builder Bruce Cowger in the bow.

Perhaps as many as 100 students were assigned in Pharaonic style to hold ropes as the new craft, sitting on a modified truck chassis, was slowly eased down the slipway. Calm seas were to be essential for safe launch and recovery, and every trip to Lundy required close monitoring of the developing weather scene and unending calculations and debate before the green light was given. Mechanical launching assistance also became necessary and, after some experimentation, the College purchased a redundant airport tractor from the nearby RAF station at St Athan.

Bruce Cowger, her principal builder, completed his two years at the College before having the chance to 'lundy' on more than one or two occasions, and his two helmsmen successors, Clifford Borg Marks from Malta and Asbjørn Damhus from Denmark, benefited from all his dedication but also spent probably hundreds of workshop hours themselves on supplementary maintenance and improvement. Bruce managed ingeniously to exploit his many hours in the workshop for academic purposes, writing his International Baccalaureate research essay on gluing techniques. Already aware that the thinners used with the Gripsotite glue also softened the surface of the hyperlon fabric, rendering it thereby more 'stickable', he established on the basis of a series of precise tests that a Surform blade, correctly applied at a series of different angles (0 degrees, 45 degrees, 90 degrees, 135 degrees), achieved superior results. This 'keying' of the surface was achieved in one quarter of the time required with hacksaw blades and achieved the vital penetration of the nylon mesh of the hyperlon without however weakening or destroying it.

X23 herself was, by Desmond Hoare's own admission, inherently a design failure. Her beam was dictated by the width of the College slipway. As a result she was too narrow for her length, a little over 30 feet, and for safety in heavy following seas. She was not a rescue boat in any sense – rather an environmental research and diving expedition vessel, driven by twin 150 hp Mercury outboard engines and carrying 100 gallons of fuel. Her limited beam meant that the engines were mounted so close to each other that one propeller would introduce turbulence and air into the other at the slightest turn. With her length roughly half a typical wave length, the stern could happily begin to surf while the bows would already be digging into the wave ahead, making her painfully subject to swinging broadside. Her student coxswains were well aware of the potential for dangerous broaching and were always on the alert. On one occasion only did things go dangerously wrong. X23 had returned to the College from Lundy late on a winter afternoon. The worsening weather made a landing on the slipway impossible. As on a number of previous occasions, the decision was made to proceed up-channel to a mooring in Barry Harbour. On the way, in total darkness near the offshore cooling tower of Aberthaw power station, the boat's nose buried itself in the wave ahead. She filled with water and almost capsized. Brought under control, the water cascading out over the stern, they went on their way, but it had been a narrow escape. On another occasion, again returning from Lundy, the engines suddenly shuddered and, on inspection, both propellers were found to have lost one blade. Here, training and preparation saved the situation. Clifford Borg Marks went over the side with tools in hand to replace the propellers with the spares carried on board, no easy task as this had to be done 'blind' in the murky, impenetrable water of the Bristol Channel, the positioning of the engines on the transom making complete lifting impossible. Happily this eventuality had been foreseen in the training programme on land.

Lundy

X23 was both the transport vehicle between St Donat's and Lundy, 40 sea miles distant, and the diving platform for all diving operations off the island. She was often out for two or three weeks at a time, far from home and servicing facilities and always afloat. The qualities that made the rigid-hulled inflatable so fine an inshore rescue craft – the high speed, the tubes for ease of coming alongside and for handling divers into and out of the water, the immediate self-draining – made her a memorable 'personality' in the early, pioneering days of the Lundy Underwater Nature Reserve. On those trips and in many different conditions including heavy swell, snow and fog, she carried a full complement of crew and divers, a full load of fuel, food supplies, a compressor, diving equipment and her own tender – the so-called 'jelly boat', alias 'X23 and a half'.

Marks McAvity, Canadian physicist and College mathematician, a former Canadian Navy diver and now the College sub-aqua instructor, was later to be deeply involved in our Canadian College's development of the Race Rocks Marine Ecological Reserve close by the College in the Straits of Juan de Fuca in

*The captivating coastline
of Lundy.*

Puget Sound in British Columbia.[14] In three years at Atlantic College he spent 70 days on Lundy. He recalls:

> *I was always struck by the fact that each time we embarked on the trip to Lundy with X23 it was a calculated tactical decision, and I often tell people that it was an interesting double approval or single veto system that the student skipper and I adopted in making decisions. If either of us was not comfortable we simply abandoned the journey. On one such occasion when 'we' agreed we could go, we stopped in Ilfracombe for a little break before heading out into the 'ocean'. While there the coast guard spotted us. It was a fairly intense fog and they clearly didn't like the fact that all these teenagers (we were fifteen I think) were heading out to the island in March in the fog. By standing up for the navigational training that the crew had had and their sense of fuel amounts and timing (including turning around if necessary and heading back to a much clearer 'target' if that proved necessary), we were 'allowed' to proceed. Though we had fog all the way we arrived dead on in the welcoming bay at Lundy and exactly on time – only to discover that the same coastguard chaps were there too.*

Clifford Borg Marks told me: *'I remember feeling extremely grateful for our training in navigation when we set out one day on a bearing to Lundy in very dense fog, and arrived exactly on target several tense hours later, thanks to the continuous directional tapping on my back by a crew member sitting behind me who spent the whole trip fixated on the compass housed between us.'*

14 www.racerocks.com

Keith Hiscock of the Lundy Field Society remembers the College students as strong-minded individuals, *'leaders rather than willing helpers'*, and their contribution to the mapping of the underwater geological formation known as the Knoll Pins as *'a brilliant contribution to increasing our knowledge of the richest area in the marine nature reserve … accurate and very competently executed … an illustration of a topographically complex feature that required in situ survey and helped to demonstrate to visiting scientists how to navigate the area and what was where by way of wildlife'*. This work was subsequently reported in the *Journal* of the Lundy Field Society. College students also carried out a survey of the bottom sediments on the east coast, working in strong cross-currents that raised all kinds of challenges in setting straight transect lines across the sea floor and in sending the core samples securely up to the surface.

An unusual feature of all this marine science activity was the training of deaf people in diving skills. This was started by Marks McAvity as a contribution to the College's now burgeoning programme of social service with the handicapped. Their ability to communicate freely underwater by the use of sign language placed them for the first time in their lives at a clear advantage over their fellows. The College student divers lost no time in acquiring these sophisticated skills themselves and found them as useful in communicating across a crowded and noisy dining hall as in carrying out survey work on the sea bed off Lundy. One of these deaf persons, Trever Draycott, a welder from Newport who had lost his hearing following childhood meningitis, became a highly valued and skilled member of many Lundy expeditions, with the disruptive tendency of telling jokes underwater which all too often compelled his fellow divers to surface in a hurry since they were unable to contain their merriment within the confines of the tight-fitting diving mask. Not long before his death he was the subject of a major BBC documentary on the problems that deaf people have in handling treatment for cancer. Others who took part in these Lundy adventures were young doctors suggested by the head of the Cardiff Hospital Accident Department, John Newham; he and his wife Kay Meller had become the College medical officers with the advent of coeducation. Their presence in these isolated circumstances was a great comfort and reassurance to all.

X23 was the main survey vessel for the Severn Barrage survey and its range in this exercise extended across the Channel east and west of Minehead and as far west as Swansea Bay on the northern side. She was also an unusual but powerful agent of public relations for the College, once giving a trip around Lundy to Sir Jack Hayward and the Liberal Party leader Jeremy Thorpe in the hope of generating some financial support for our Lundy efforts from the wealthy Jack Hayward.

On another occasion, Thor Heyerdahl came to visit St Donat's. He was taken out and subjected to some 'bouncing around' on the erratic waves generated by the rip currents off the Nash Sands. His deadpan response to the invitation, on the way back to the slipway, to comment on her qualities was unexpected: *'I prefer rafts!'* But when he was assembling the crew for his raft **Tigris** in 1978 for his 6,800-kilometre voyage down Shatt-el-Arab in Iraq to the Persian Gulf, out into the Indian Ocean, then via Muscat in Oman to the Indus Valley in Pakistan, before finally leaving Asia and across the Indian Ocean to Africa, he took Asbjørn Damhus with him in his crew. This was fitting recognition of Asbjørn's impressive record in maintaining X23 in seaworthy condition and his leadership in the many challenging situations he faced on journeys between the College and Lundy and at Lundy itself. The most notable was when he and his crew were moving X23 to the south of Lundy to find shelter from an easterly gale. When first one and then the other engine stopped, they were forced to anchor to avoid being swept out to sea by the strong outgoing tide. Whilst trying to restart the engines he noticed that a crew member appeared to have lost consciousness and indeed could not be roused despite being placed in an exposure bag. A helicopter was called for by radio and lifted off the crew member. Subsequently, no reason for his drowsy state could be identified. X23 herself was towed into a safe position by the **Polar Bear**, the regular Lundy supply vessel, lifted on to the deck and transported back to Ilfracombe. Asbjørn was in good Atlantic College company on Thor Heyerdahl's raft – another former student, Hans Peter Bohn from Norway, was also selected for the crew.

The exposed mooring off Lundy led to a series of narrow escapes from overnight disaster, and engine problems made return to Ilfracombe necessary aboard the **Polar Bear** on more than one occasion. X23 was eventually lost in a rare northerly gale whilst moored off Lundy's east coast. The island offers fine shelter from easterly and westerly but not from northerly winds. X23 was overturned at her mooring in the night by the violence of the storm and the anchor cleat, now placed under strain from an unplanned angle, gave way. Thus she became another in the long line of Lundy wrecks but had the distinction of contributing with her scarred wooden hull to the beacon lit on Lundy for the Queen's Silver Jubilee – a Viking funeral with a difference.

Lundy remains, in 2010, Britain's only Marine Nature Reserve. Just 0.01% of British coastal waters are as fully protected as the waters around this island.

Thor Heyerdahl's crew for his raft Tigris. *Hans Peter Bohn and Asbjørn Damhus in the front row on the right, Asbjørn in the Atlantic College sweater.*

CHAPTER 15
The Rigid Inflatable Today

The opening paper in the 2005 Conference of the Royal Institution of Naval Architects stated that it was *'probably safe to say that the development of the RIB has been the most significant design development in the small craft area over the past 50 years'*. The representative of British Petroleum told the same conference, referring to safety operations in the offshore energy industry, that

> recovery of survivors by fast rescue craft is generally acknowledged to be by far and away the most practical option, and properly trained personnel have safely carried out rescue missions in quite severe weather conditions … in all such operations craft of the RIB type play an essential role and many of the activities referred to in this paper would be difficult or impossible without such craft being available.

Rigid-inflatable boats are indeed now found the world over. As rescue craft they are as ubiquitous in national life-saving societies as in offshore energy exploration. Few national military forces are without them. They are used for smuggling and for drug trafficking and for the policing of these activities alike. They have become powerful, highly sophisticated racing craft. And they continue to serve as

A Haitian boy watches as rigid-hull inflatable boats from the amphibious dock landing ships arrive ashore at the New Hope Mission at Bonel, Haiti. This was one of many relief projects initiated after the earthquake disaster of 12 January 2010.

The Italian Falco (Falcon) Class RIB, 10.4 metres in length, with a range of 250 nautical miles at 35 knots and a top speed of 54 knots, is used by the Guardia di Finanza (Tax and Customs Police).

pleasure boats, as tenders for yachts, in support of diving activities, and in their own right as handy, speedy, seaworthy run-abouts, cruising and expedition craft.

The US Coastguard has recently placed a contract for 700 8-metre RIBs and is replacing all their 42-foot Utility Boats with a 14-metre RIB design.

Rigid-hulled inflatables have now been built with speeds of over 100 knots.

One of the most advanced RIBs ever built has been a 55 footer powered by 4 × 1000-hp diesels.

FB Design in Italy has created a 60-knot fast rescue craft that may become the basis of a new generation of high speed all-weather lifeboats.

Experiments are under way with a hybrid catamaran hull form, which suggests that Charles Vintner's **Hydrocar** of 1965 may not have been too far off the mark after all. The so-called SledCat, targeted primarily at military and specific commercial roles, stands upright unsupported on a beach, and has a high load-carrying capacity, a large deck area and the potential to off-load both fore and aft. However, the strongly diminished role of the tube raises doubts about its status as a rigid-hulled inflatable.

In South Africa in particular, experimentation has been taking place with a hydrofoil-supported rigid inflatable. The largest **Hysucat** (hydro-supported catamaran), as reported to the RINA Conference in 2005,[15] is the 45-metre E-Cat developed by Halter Marine in New Orleans; the smallest, the 6.5-metre semi-rigid inflatable of Stealth Marine in Gordon's Bay, South Africa. Already in 1998, this 6.5-metre version had taken part in the Trans Agulhas Inflatable Race over 1,000 kilometres along the southern coast of South Africa. By 2005 more than 400 boats had been produced. With twin 50 hp outboard engines they reach speeds of 50 knots in open sea conditions. Not only Atlantic College students will be struck by the wave spoiler system which prevents excessive bow dipping when running in heavy following seas, and by the critical role of the spray rails in controlling the vortex created by water impact, thereby ensuring a softer ride. Outboard engines with automatic trim permit optimum trim of the craft itself in accordance with the sea conditions, the prevailing load and the speed, all with push-button control. The standard production RIB with the thicker and stronger main foil, which also allows beaching, has top speeds of between 36 and 40 knots and can carry up to ten persons. An improved version, initiated in 1999, saw an 8-metre RIB with 150 hp XR 2 Mercury racing engines and 28-inch pitch cleaver surface piercing propellers and a special 5-degree dihedral foil achieve speeds over 70 knots in a later Trans Agulhas race.

Numerous new types of hull construction have also evolved. These have taken advantage of advanced composites such as epoxy resin, sandwich construction and carbon reinforcement as well as, in many cases, aluminium. The opportunities of creating lighter and stiffer hulls, capable of a higher performance, have had to be reconciled with production costs that have centred on the cost of materials and the number of man hours required both in manufacture and subsequent maintenance. The lighter, less cluttered hulls have made possible greater freedom in internal layout and for increased ancillary equipment. This general process is exemplified by the experimental work that led to the hulls for the new RNLI 8.5 metre. The first two prototypes were built using glass-reinforced fibre outer skins and carbon inner skins for the hull and deck. The internal structure consisted of four transverse frames with two longitudinals each side of the boat. Subsequent boats used carbon reinforcement throughout the boat, which allowed the internal structure to be reduced to one longitudinal each side. The final outcome was an RIB prototype some 20% larger than the previous inshore lifeboat with a 20% reduction in structural weight, capable of production at comparable cost.

And just as the hulls have benefited from the adoption and use of new materials, so too the tubes have come under scrutiny and experimentation. One adaptation by a Scottish firm, in response to the fish farming industry and its need to handle cumbersome and heavy equipment in all weathers, has been the development of RIBs with hard polyethylene tubular collars, with very satisfactory results. The

15 The details in this and the following paragraph are taken from the Report of the Royal Institution of Naval Architects on their Conference on Rigid Inflatables, held in June 2005 in Cowes. Such is the pace of development in these matters that they are certain to have been overtaken by more recent innovations.

new possibilities offered by tubes capable with handling pressures unimaginable in the days when the College students at sea pumped up their tubes, which had deflated and gone limp as they entered the cold water, have led some to underline and regret the inability of the new tubes to play their part in absorbing the energy of the sea. Do we now have rigid-hulled rigid-tubed inflatables? Indeed we do. A company in Australia, Orca Boats, is making them and calls them RBBs – rigid buoyancy boats!

Atlantic College students – remembering the acute discomforts of the early days, the cold wet hours on the Bristol Channel, the difficulties of 'hanging on' in rough seas, the tensions, perhaps even the fear, of confronting the massive tides and currents – will be impressed to know that, as these new, sophisticated, ever faster planing boats impose comparisons with aircraft rather than with larger sea-going vessels, there is an unmistakeable emphasis on *'human factor design standards'*. *'Unintuitive (navigational) displays which require excessive cognitive work'* are being improved to permit a higher degree of *'coxswain skills … including psycho-motor skills … and cognitive processing'* to enhance performance, especially during operations at night and in periods of *'degraded situational awareness'*. It is not only the boats that have become more complex. In rather more accessible language, the helmsmen of these craft are now being asked to develop some of the qualities of riders of powerful motor cycles and of highly competitive downhill skiers.

The Dutch 19-metre Arie Visser in action.

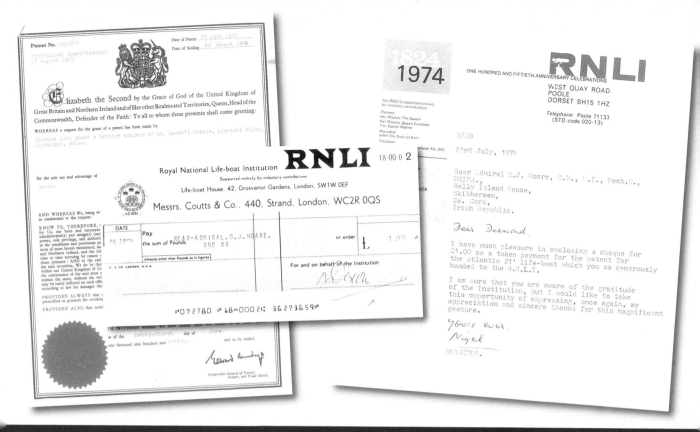

Postscript

And so finally to the inevitable question. Was the concept ever patented; and was there a financial benefit to the College?

The answer is as improbable as the fact that the whole affair originated in a school, but it fully reflects the spirit in which it all happened.

After the French company Zodiac had sent a director to Atlantic College in 1965/6 to look at the work going on there, the design was patented in France but not, it later transpired, in Britain. Desmond Hoare eventually made an application in June 1970, and a British patent was finally granted on 24th January 1973. But in May 1972 he had already told the Avon Company that they could have commercial use of any future patent rights *'in return for a reasonable donation to the RNLI'*. The word *'reasonable'* was never defined. In 1974 Desmond received a cheque from the RNLI dated 18th July for £1.00 in *'token payment for the patent for the Atlantic 21 which you so generously handed to the RNLI'*. He never cashed it.

In 1974 he and Naomi retired to an extremely modest cottage in County Cork, severely strapped for funds owing to the pension sacrifices he had made when leaving the Navy early. There they were fortified principally by a steady stream of visits from loyal former students. Desmond was by now convinced that the United World Colleges must make their mark in developing countries if they were to remain true to their and Hahn's ideals of rescue and service. He was strongly critical of the failure of the UWC to support and join the one inter-denominational school in Belfast, Logan College. He and Naomi kept their boating interests alive through their involvement in the activities of the local RNLI and sailing club. Had he still been at the College he would have been captivated by the proposal made to the College to run a rigid-hulled inflatable across the Atlantic; and he would have been fascinated too by the suggestion of the visiting Astronomer Royal and Nobel Prize winner in Physics, Sir Martin Ryle, that the College should develop self-inflating collars for ocean-going yachts to act as life-belts for them in extreme emergency; he would have started the design work the same evening. As it was, a former student, whose parents lived nearby in County Cork, recalls Desmond building, at a neighbour's request, what must have been the smallest ever rigid-hulled inflatable, a combination tender and life raft some 8 feet in length and fairly rounded:

> It had a tube all the way round, a centre board and a mast arrangement so you could sail it. There must have been some sort of rudder attachment – in fact I seem to remember that you could attach the rudder to either end ... I have a vague memory that Desmond entered the design in some form of competition. I certainly think the project was written up in an article for one of the yachting magazines.

Alas, Desmond was laid low by severe illness in his final years before dying in 1988.

One publication[16] on the rigid-hulled inflatable, whilst warmly acknowledging that no other *'singleton'* has *'simultaneously found favour with the Royal Navy, the US Coastguard, military agencies, the North Sea oil industry, police, divers, off-shore racers, the RNLI and many other professional and leisure users'*, was also keen to point out that *'nobody sat to a drawing board with the set intention of designing this marvellous piece of equipment as a conceptual, "ab initio" marine project.'* Are there any boats in the history of mankind which have emerged in so theoretical, predetermined a way? The same publication, which convincingly draws attention to the *'accidents, problems, solutions ... and necessities'* that formed the history of these craft, appropriately gives credit to *'some very sound seafaring imagination'*.

Looking back, it is reasonably clear that the innovations achieved by the Atlantic College under Desmond Hoare's leadership achieved their final stage with X7 and X8 in 1968: fast, manoeuvrable, outstandingly seaworthy boats with strong hulls, tubes designed for the purpose, seats that enabled two crew to operate in reasonable comfort and with excellent all-round vision (a third crew member still tube-riding), room for a stretcher, reel and line for the recovery of

16 *Rigid Inflatable Boats* by Colin Jones, Waterline Books, 1992.

casualties inside the surf line, radio, navigation and other lights for night operation, good first aid equipment, an emergency cut-off switch for the engine, and crew members possessing a full range of swimming, life-saving, first aid, sailing and canoeing qualifications. The **Psychedelic Surfer** adventure of 1969 was the critical event that confirmed the rigid-hull inflatable's potential to the RNLI, the marine world and the public at large. It was a huge advance in just over six years of intensive adventure and extremely hard work. The extraordinary developments that have taken place since then have quite naturally been achieved by the RNLI, by fellow life-saving societies such as the Dutch, by commercial organisations including pre-eminently those in the offshore energy business worldwide, and by marine enthusiasts of all kinds with perhaps a special emphasis on those in the racing world. Professional resources and expertise have led to astonishing new features that have met widely varying specific needs and ambitions and have also drawn on the impressive range of modern materials and constructional methods made possible by these materials and by modern research. But all who have the name of the Atlantic College in their hearts will be grateful for the degree of recognition accorded it first and foremost by the RNLI itself but also by many others for the achievements of those formative years 1962 to 1969.

Desmond Hoare was not a great reader but he read thoroughly. He used to say that one long and serious book was as much as he could digest properly in a summer vacation. One year he took with him to his little cottage in Ireland Arthur Koestler's *The Act of Creation* and he sometimes referred to it afterwards. It happens to contain a rather appropriate comment on the nature of his achievement: '*the more original a discovery, the more obvious it seems afterwards. The creative act ... does not create something out of nothing; it uncovers, selects, reshuffles, combines, synthesises ... the more familiar the parts, the more striking the new whole ... the Latin verb cogito for "to think" means "to shake together".*' Relevant too are

The new College RNLI Station is dedicated in their presence to Desmond and Naomi Hoare in May 1983.

131

More exciting than
motor cycles!

the words of Pasteur about himself, also quoted by Koestler: '*Fortune favours the prepared mind!*'

And is it not the case that the practical philosophies and practices of the Atlantic College under Desmond's leadership continue to have profound meaning and value in education? Willem de Vogel remembers: '*I feel today that my two-year involvement with the RNLI and the Atlantic College ILB programme under the guidance of Admiral Hoare had the greatest impact on me of all "education" I received.*' Some impact! When he saw an early draft of this book Willem, a senior and successful merchant banker of many years' standing in the United States, insisted that his X8 did 36, not 34 knots! Another student who attended the College after Desmond Hoare's departure wrote: '*A number of us double-dyed ILB'ers … quite deliberately limited our academic efforts in favour of boats. We were freer then, had responsibilities, authority and did something real and useful. It wasn't a bad bargain in the end.*' A later engineer made this professional comment:

Looking back, it seems to me that the AC rescue boat set-up was a wonderful example of a prototype testing operation … a couple of months of operation amounted to a vast quantity of experience and fatigue testing of the boats. The evolution of the X-boats was a great example of incremental engineering, enabling the type to be rapidly developed, with a relatively mature design appearing much more quickly than would have otherwise been the case.

And one of those who was in at the very beginning, also a rescue boater, said: '*I realise that the most precious thing that Atlantic College (and Desmond Hoare) gave me was the certainty that it was necessary and worthwhile to buck the trend, to hold out for a vision of how things could be done better and not to settle for the predictable, comfortable option.*'

In a House of Lords debate on 7th February 1968 the Atlantic College was mentioned twice. On the second occasion Lord Hunt, the leader of the successful Everest expedition in 1953, later the Director of the Duke of Edinburgh's Award Scheme, referred to '*the splendid rescue services in which the Atlantic College at St Donat's Castle in South Wales sets an outstanding example. Facing up to danger is a worthy experience for youth.*'

The Duke of Edinburgh had written to Kurt Hahn on 21st April 1964 after his first visit:

> *There is no doubt in my mind that the single greatest influence at the College is the responsibility for preventing loss of life along that part of the coast. The most discouraging aspect of the problem of young people in Britain is the almost universal refusal to give them any real responsibility. I admit that my experience is limited but I have yet to hear of any serious case of failure to respond to responsibility or to measure up to the responsibility imposed upon a young person.*

Amen!

The Atlantic College Inshore Life Boat Station 1964–2008:

Launches on service	434 of which 107 at night
Crew hours at sea	1,622 – this figure does not include crew in College boats assisting the official RNLI craft
Lives saved	97
Fatalities	35
Persons recovered unharmed	103
Persons recovered injured	9
College students injured	0

Appendix 1

A summary of the Atlantic College contribution to the design of the rigid-hulled inflatable by the former student David Riley (1965–7)

My impressions at the time and to this day are of evolutionary change from the pure inflatable design where the tube is the primary feature to the eventual designs where the hull is dominant and the tube became an almost ancillary item. It's as though the floor sections of the early Zodiacs and Avons grew and metamorphosed into conventional speedboat hulls. This process occurred in a series of stages which can be tracked from one AC prototype to another.

The evolutionary approach kept many a student usefully occupied but a more detached observer may have short-circuited the process. The projects were valuable educationally, bore useful fruit and I imagine cost the RNLI relatively little. From a commercial perspective, however, I suspect the process could have been telescoped into a shorter time period had commercial companies made greater financial investments.

The tube of a true inflatable provides buoyancy and much of the strength, shape and integrity of the boat, although removable floor sections provide an essential backbone. In the rigid-hulled inflatable the primary buoyancy, shape and integrity is provided by the hull and the tube provides secondary buoyancy.

The major trends in AC's prototype, marine-ply hull designs were:

The hulls became wider as time went by, to lift the tubes out of the water and to minimise hydrodynamic drag.

The hulls became deeper at the transom, providing greater buoyancy for increasingly powerful and heavy engines.

The transom became lower and eventually a narrow stump, to permit rapid self-drainage of the deck (in parallel with increases to hull depth at the transom).

The hulls grew larger and heavier as concerns about portability (an attraction of true inflatables) lost their initial importance.

The filling of hull sections with polyurethane foam blocks was abandoned.

The bows became sharper in plan and the taper extended further down the hull to streamline the shape.

The hull decking went from a plane to a curved surface with a pronounced lift at the bow.

The driving position changed from the rear tube to a seat further forward and the use of a steering wheel to improve visibility and trim (especially when rising on to the plane) but at the cost of greater weight and mechanical complexity.

The major trends in the tubes were:

The tubes became more sophisticated, three-dimensional shapes to reflect the changing relationships with the hull.

The tubes became sharper towards the bow and had a pronounced lift so the sections were no longer in a single plane.

The tubes were originally attached around and overhanging the hull, where they were in continuous contact with the water, but later moved on top of and almost inside the hull.

Appendix 2

An account by Peter Jolley of the development of the College crane equipment for cliff rescue

Before Atlantic College opened I was interviewed for a post in the old London Office in Denmark House, and towards the end of the interview I was asked: 'As a rock climber; what is your reaction to limestone cliffs with shale bedding planes?' and without hesitation I replied: 'Leave well alone.' In spite of this remark, however, I found myself the following August surveying those self-same cliffs in order to decide whether a cliff rescue technique was possible without undue risk to the operating team. I can well remember how terrified I was of the damp rubble of these cliffs compared with the good sound rock on which I had previously climbed ... We also surveyed the cliff tops for belaying points and were dismayed to find that, apart from two small stretches, there was precious little to tie a rope to along nine miles of cliff ... There were numerous vertical faults even in the coastal bays and the headland points were so unstable as to be suicidal to the climber. For about thirty feet at the base of the cliff the rock was weathered by the sea and was smooth and firm but the top twenty feet of any cliff is very unstable indeed. Water draining from the land makes this section wet and very loose. In wet and frosty weather large sections break away from the top and in dry seasons the shale bands become powdery and produce a rain of smaller stones when disturbed. Because of wave action at the base this kind of cliff is always overhanging ...

As a result of this preliminary survey it became clear that any rescue technique must take account of three basic principles.

Wherever possible the headlands should be avoided, certainly for training purposes as the rock is highly unstable. Fortunately most cliff accidents occur in the bays as people who are cut off by the tide are forced into these areas.

Strains must be avoided on the lip of the cliff at the top.

A method needs to be evolved that keeps the rescuer and casualty away from the cliff face. Where contact is made with the cliff face, pressures must be inwards at right angles to the face, pushing loose rock into the cliff. Sheering stresses along the cliff face must be avoided.

It was the second of these principles (beware of the lip of the cliff) that prompted the decision to avoid the use of wire ladders which are used by many rescue organisations including the fire service. Ladders place the maximum strain on the cliff edge directly above the casualty and rescuer and they are also very difficult to negotiate on long overhangs. Also ladders need the use of two hands which should be available to tend to the casualty for at least part of the time. All these considerations convinced me that there was a better solution than the use of flexible ladders.

The third basic principle (keep away from the face) forced us to consider the design of some sort of crane or boom to carry ropes and rescuers well out from the cliff, thus enabling the only contact to be via the feet, used as buffers, and pressing inwards flat on the cliff surface, but never downwards with a shearing strain. The preliminary survey work took about six months and all this time we were discussing ideas about cranes and hoists, but the most urgent unsolved problem was how to secure any equipment to the cliff top. We had tried hammering stakes into the cliff top but the average depth of soil was four inches and driving through the underlying rock was a lengthy business … we therefore decided to write to a wide range of firms concerned with mountaineering and civil engineering for suggestions. The answer came from a Sheffield company who introduced us to the Molex ground anchor. This is a German invention which is virtually a large screw which is twisted into the ground by two people using a bar. It will penetrate loose rock and will hold in shallow soil. With three Molex anchors in a triangle we had six tons of ground anchorage and a splendid fixed point for our equipment. The same firm also sent details of the Tirfor Hoist which we were to adopt as our lifting device to pull rescuers and casualties up the cliff on a wire cable. We made a number of visits to the Civil Defence in Bridgend to see this hoist used in the rescue of victims under fallen masonry before we adapted it for our equipment.

After about twelve months of investigations it seemed to me that we were ready to put some of our ideas to the test of slide rule and calculation and we began to search for an engineer who would help us to design a crane … after some persuasion the Managing Director, Mr Able of Lyte Ladders, became enthusiastic about our plans and helped to design the first cliff rescue crane. Our specifications to him were:

The crane should have a swinging boom to carry a load bearing cable well away from the cliff edge and it should be able to swing a casualty over the lip of the cliff without disturbing the friable rock at the edge.

The crane should be sectional and easily portable by a team of ten students.

The whole equipment was to have a very generous safety margin in terms of operating stresses and strength of materials.

The Mark 1 crane was made of mild steel and it was only just portable by a team of very large students. Over longish distances the team was in need of revival on arrival at the cliff and it was clear after a period of usage that the safety factor of the equipment was unnecessarily large. We had a great deal of fun, exercise and nervous strain learning to handle this first crane as a team. Firstly we spent a number of afternoons handling it in the middle of a field. Then we moved it to a flat cliff top and eventually we erected it on the cliffs near Southerndown where the cliff top slopes at forty-five degrees to the edge. This was a very exciting period of pushing the team into increasingly difficult situations and all the time insisting on very strict safeguards to protect the team against any failure of the untested equipment. I still marvel at the degree of precision and team work needed in cliff rescue. It would have been so easy to drop a piece of equipment over the edge but apart from an occasional helmet or glove it never happened … we returned to Mr Able with a list of observations and frustrations and he designed the Mark 2 crane made of aluminium alloy with nylon bushes for moving parts …

After two years of operation … two outstanding problems needed further attention.

Firstly, vertical communication, especially on high overhanging cliffs, was very difficult. We had adopted coloured ropes for identification but the code of whistle signals which we used was barely adequate in a wind or where a complex rescue situation was involved. The introduction of VHF radio sets went a long way to solving these difficulties, but I believe there is a need to experiment in methods of carrying these sets in cliff rescue. They need to be designed as an integral part of the rescue harness and the ear piece and microphone should be built into the helmet of the rescuer …

Secondly, there were early problems concerned with the comfort of the rescuer and casualty while on the cliff face. In the early days the rescuer descended the cliff by a sling and karabiner abseil and this regularly produced the trade mark of crossed rope burns across the back. The adoption of the Pierre Allain Descendeur helped to ease this problem. However, rope discomfort can be acute if one has to remain on the cliff face for up to half an hour and during the first year of the unit we began to experiment with home made parachute harnesses and eventually adopted a safety harness manufactured by G. K. Parachutes. This enables the rescuer to sit comfortably with the feet flat on the cliff and with the hands completely free to manage ropes and casualty …

In the third year of the unit an approach was made to HM Coastguard to ask whether we would be acceptable as an auxiliary Coastguard Unit. The unit had been used once or twice in salvage operations with the College boats and it seemed reasonable that we would be more general value if we combined cliff techniques with some skills in shore to ship rescue. We began a most enjoyable initial training course with HM Coastguard from both the Swansea and Llantwit Major stations and at the end of a good deal of hard work and good humour we were appointed an auxiliary coastguard station. In this connection we not only acquired new skills but also an entirely new nautical vocabulary, both official and unofficial.

Thus after three years the cliff rescue unit had adopted a five point training programme:

Basic Rock and Rope Work
First Aid Training
Cliff Rescue Techniques
Shore to Ship Rescue
Equipment Maintenance and Design

Appendix 3

Some Atlantic College students were stimulated by their experiences on the Bristol Channel to become marine engineers. David Nockels attended the College in 1969–71 and was the captain of X9 and the Secretary of the Inshore Rescue Boat Unit in his second year. He returned on many occasions thereafter to work on the boats and helped the then students in the early construction of X23. After leaving the College he studied naval architecture and marine engineering, becoming a chartered engineer and naval architect. He has spent many years as a safety and risk engineer in locations across the world, especially in the offshore oil and gas industry, where he has helped develop improved offshore rescue systems. He has led research projects for the UK Department of Energy and the UK Health and Safety Executive and acted as a consultant to various oil companies and industry trade associations He is also a professional helicopter pilot. In the contribution that follows, David illustrates the remarkable manner in which those early Atlantic College boats have, in the hands of professional designers, become a key, highly sophisticated tool for a world energy company in maintaining safety for its offshore employees.

Completing the Jigsaw – the British Petroleum Story by David Nockels

BP has designed a super-RIB for rescue and recovery in the UK offshore oil and gas industry. Known as an Autonomous Rescue and Recovery Craft (ARRC), it provides an essential part of their JIGSAW rescue and recovery system for their many UK sector offshore installations. In the ARRC the RIB has been developed and refined from its early form. At the same time, the fundamental characteristics and benefits of the RIB still provide a true advantage over other boat types.

1. **Derivation of the ARRC Design Requirement**
   a. The UK Requirements for Offshore Installation Rescue and Recovery
      The explosion on the ***Piper Alpha*** offshore platform in 1988 with the loss of 167 lives changed completely the way in which offshore oil and gas operations were managed and controlled. It enabled a thoroughly innovative approach to be adopted for the provision of rescue and recovery arrangements.

      Before ***Piper Alpha*** there had been a prescriptive regulatory safety regime. The regulations imposed very specific and detailed requirements on the operators of the offshore installations.

      The original regulations for rescue and recovery required that each offshore installation be provided with a standby vessel (SBV). Each SBV had one or more fast-rescue craft (almost always RIBs), to be the primary means of response for rescue and recovery. The standards of the SBV and its equipment were closely defined in the relevant requirements, but there was very little room for innovation.

      The Cullen Inquiry, which investigated ***Piper Alpha***, led to a complete change of the method of regulation. This has had a significant effect on all aspects of the safety of these operations, but in particular the arrangements for emergency evacuation, recovery and rescue.

The post-Piper regime set various safety goals to be achieved by the offshore installation and its support facilities. Each installation was to be the subject of a documented safety case. In it the operator had to demonstrate that the goals were satisfied for the particular installation. In respect of Emergency Response and particularly rescue and recovery, the goals were set as follows:

The duty holder shall ensure that effective arrangements are made, which include such arrangements with suitable persons beyond the installation, for:
* *Recovery of persons following their evacuation or escape from the installation;*
* *Rescue of persons near the installation;*
* *Taking such persons to a Place of Safety.*

Arrangements were regarded as being effective if they secured a good prospect of being rescued or recovered to a place of safety.

b. The BP Jigsaw Project

Given the above requirements, BP determined to address and improve rescue and recovery for all its UK installations together via the **Jigsaw Project**, rather than for each installation in isolation. Taking account of the location of their various installations they decided to provide dedicated Search and Rescue helicopters, including one based offshore on an installation, the Miller platform. Various marine vessels supplemented these aircraft to give the necessary overall coverage, capacity, system availability, rapid and appropriate response and all-weather capability. Where a number of installations were located close together a combination of Region Support Vessels (RSV) and ARRCs was decided upon. The RSV was a large vessel intended to provide emergency response and support to a number of installations. Each RSV had 2 ARRCs. The ARRCs were launched and recovered using specially designed davits.

The overall system design generated 3 key *Performance Standards* (PS) relevant to the ARRC:
* For *close-standby* the first casualty into the water must be recovered in 4 minutes and the last of four in 10 minutes. All 4 are to be in a place of safety within 20 minutes. [Close-standby is when a vessel or craft stations itself close to an installation. It is required when installation workers are working overside or doing other work where man-overboard from a substantial height is more likely. Such workers are likely to suffer from cold shock on water entry and to be injured in the course of entering the water and will not normally wear immersion suits, so rapid rescue is vital.]
* For helicopter ditching, all persons must be recovered to a place of safety within 2 hours of entering the water. [In this case, rescue vessels and SAR helicopters may be some way from the scene. All helicopter personnel will be trained in helicopter underwater escape training and will be wearing immersion suits, extending their in-water survival time.]
* For a major installation incident, where total installation evacuation may be required, all persons must be recovered to a place of safety within 2 hours of entering the water. [Again, rescue vessels and SAR helicopters may be some way from the scene. Most personnel in a planned evacuation to the sea will be wearing immersion suits, extending their in-water survival time.]

In order to fulfil these Performance Standards the ARRC will need to have certain capabilities. The more important of these are:

Extreme Sea-keeping: If the ARRCs are to be relied upon to recover or rescue people from the sea within the Performance Standards times, then they must be able to do this in severe sea states and poor weather. This requires the best possible sea keeping capability, the ability to maintain speed and to launch and recover using the RSV davits.

Autonomous Operations: The ARRC will have to be able to operate autonomously from the RSV to:

- Provide close-standby for overside working for extended periods remote from the RSV; **and**
- Enable it to operate as a rapidly available Place of Safety for platform evacuation remote from the RSV.

Place of Safety: It was a key requirement that the ARRC could be shown to be a Place of Safety, as defined.

These capabilities were critical in shaping the design and operation of the ARRC.

2. **The ARRC (Autonomous Rescue and Recovery Craft)**

The ARRC RIB is a large (18 m LOA), high-speed (35 knots max) deep-V planing hull. Its hull form is based upon a well-established family of Delta RIB hulls with the same proportions, but has been scaled up to be a larger vessel. The hull is a foam-reinforced plastic sandwich construction. It is fitted with an enclosed accommodation two-deck superstructure that is air-conditioned and includes a casualty treatment area. The superstructure acts in several ways:

- To protect the crew and any casualties from the environment;
- To provide self-righting capability in the same way as modern RNLI lifeboats;
- To provide a raised location from which to more easily locate casualties in the sea.

The craft carries a crew of 6 and is designed to have a survivor capacity of 25, but is able physically to receive up to 84.

2 Caterpillar C18 engines (18 litres and 1,000 bhp) power the ARRC through Hamilton water-jets with a joystick control.

The davits fitted to the RSV were specially designed for the ARRC. They were designed and demonstrated to be able to allow the ARRCs to be launched and recovered in sea states up to 7/5 metre significant wave height respectively. This is significantly better than previous combinations. The davits also need to be able to operate reliably as they are used routinely, not just for emergency launches. This improvement in launch and recovery performance is critical to satisfying the Performance Standards.

The sponson has grown in size with the rest of the craft, so that recovering survivors over them would not be a practical proposition. A feature of the design is a removable section of tube and deck edge towards the stern. Once this is removed survivors can be rescued in the gap in the sponson. The sealed rigid hull maintains stability with the sponson element removed.

a. The ARRC Design and Development Process

Unlike the development of RIBs at Atlantic College, it is not practical to conduct design and development through the use of sequential full-size prototypes for such a large and expensive craft. The full range of normal prediction methods available to modern naval architecture was used as well as some unusual methods. In total, these included:

- Craft scale model testing for hydrodynamic resistance and powering, sea-keeping and aerodynamic wind tunnel testing;
- Sea-keeping and slamming acceleration testing was completed using an 8.4 m hull from the Delta range;
- Computer and physical simulations to model the impact forces, motions and accelerations imposed on the hull, its occupants and equipment fitted on the ARRC;
- A full range of computer analysis using the various conventional modern software packages available to naval architects.

Some particularly noteworthy work and results arose from this process. These included:

i) The optimisation of sea-keeping capability allowed the ARRC to be able to maintain a speed of 25 knots whilst planing in seas as large as 7-metre significant wave height – a major achievement.

ii) The re-design of crew impact-absorbing seats to provide much greater protection to the crew. This allowed the RIB to maintain speed in rough seas without risking injury to the crew.

iii) The treatment area and equipment were optimised to allow casualty treatment, despite the motions and impacts to be expected in a vessel in a seaway.

iv) The adoption of the engine/water-jet propulsion and control system provides an extremely manoeuvrable vessel.

b. Helpful RIB Characteristics

In the design and subsequent use of the ARRC various RIB characteristics were particularly beneficial:

- The rigid hull is essential to achieving the high levels of planing sea-keeping performance that were achieved;
- The sponson assisted in reducing peak slamming and accelerations by damping the pitch and heave motions found in a planing powerboat in a sea way;
- The sponson is also of great assistance in the process of going alongside the RSV and launching and recovering from and to it;
- The compartmentalisation and reserve buoyancy inherent in a RIB would undoubtedly assist in any extreme or accidental loss of stability or buoyancy event.

Reference

Fryer D, Gorrie J, Graville P, Pieces of a Jigsaw – The Development of BP's New Platform Support and Rescue System for the North Sea, *Journal of Ocean Technology*, Vol. 2, No. 42007

Appendix 4

THE UNITED WORLD COLLEGES AND THE INTERNATIONAL BACCALAUREATE

International education made a hesitant start in the aftermath of the First World War, its most prominent and longest surviving protagonist being the International School of Geneva, launched against the idealistic but ill-fated background of the League of Nations.

The story after the Second World War has been dramatically different. The threatening scenario of the Cold War, combined with accelerating commercial and other cooperation in the western world, stimulated two organisations to lay a path now followed by thousands of both international and national (state) schools. The organisations were the United World Colleges and the International Baccalaureate.

Reforming, high quality academic performance, a wholehearted commitment to an education in active citizenship through activities and community services that foster personal responsibility, and leadership in securing the recognition of a single diploma for university entry worldwide – these have been the defining features and achievements.

The Atlantic College Project, renamed the United World Colleges (UWC) in 1968, has branched out in important ways from the initial concept of a two-year sixth-form course. Whilst all but one of their members follow the programmes of the International Baccalaureate (IB), some are all-age schools and one is vocational and post-secondary. They are linked by a common philosophy in which active service to the community is the overriding theme. National committees of volunteers across the world raise funds and select students. There is a coordinating head office in London. Governance is in the hands of a board of directors and the UWC International Council. UWC teachers continue to play an important role in developing syllabuses for the IB, in leading teacher workshops and in acting as examiners. Scholarship programmes make it possible for the majority of students entering the colleges offering only the two-year course to be selected on merit and potential, irrespective of race, religion and financial background – indeed, certain colleges will not accept parental contributions. Smaller numbers of similar scholarship students enter the other colleges.

Past International Presidents of the UWC International Council have been Earl Mountbatten of Burma and HRH The Prince of Wales. The current President is Queen Noor of Jordan. Nelson Mandela is the Honorary President.

UNITED WORLD COLLEGES OFFERING TWO-YEAR COURSES

United World College of the Atlantic (1962)

The first decade of the College was marked by its struggle for financial survival and by its remarkable development of the concept of coast rescue by teenagers. The accomplishment of its second decade was its total commitment to the successful introduction, development and propagation of the IB. With the gradual withdrawal of Desmond Hoare from the affairs of the College, marine activities inescapably lost much of their impetus. The setting up of the National Coast Rescue Training Centre in nearby Aberavon removed from the College the focus on the rescue training of young people from across Britain, but the College's wider obligations to society were fulfilled with the creation of the Extra-Mural Centre, housed in the restored cavalry barracks by the sea front. This centre has since provided courses for many local community groups, including young offenders, unemployed people on government training schemes, those with disabilities and the infirm. Current students and former students are the principal instructors and assistants on all these courses. In addition, many local schools benefit from a close association with the College.

Perhaps inevitably, financial problems were to return. Not only were British local education authorities, the main sponsors of British students, no longer able to allocate scholarship funds; but also the new colleges began to impose severe burdens on hard-pressed UWC National Committees, who were now being asked to send students to several rather than just one or two colleges. The Atlantic College is in the unique position of being the founder mother college of the entire UWC movement, a heavy but honourable burden. Its achievements will be celebrated in 2012, its fiftieth anniversary.

Lester B. Pearson United World College of the Pacific, British Columbia, Canada (1974)

The former NATO Secretary-General, Canadian Prime Minister and Nobel Peace Prize winner visited the Atlantic College twice in its early years. After his death his family and the Canadian government agreed that a College on Vancouver Island should become his principal memorial. It has benefited from generous support from both governmental and private sources and has set its fellow colleges exacting expectations with its 100% scholarship policy that excludes all parental contributions. Its stewardship of the Race Rocks Marine Nature Reserve in the San Juan Straits has earned both national and international recognition.

United World College – USA, New Mexico (1982)

Several failed attempts in the 1970s to assign the United States a major role with the creation of a College were eventually successful when Armand Hammer, applying ruthless business drive, commissioned the identification, renovation and launch of the legendary old 'castle' of Montezuma as the home of the movement's second College in North America. Armand Hammer, who at a critical moment was also a benefactor of the IB, also provided endowment funding in the early years. The College been in the forefront – not only within the UWC movement – of the promotion of conflict resolution techniques, 'the constructive engagement of conflict', in education.

United World College of the Adriatic, Friuli-Venezia Giulia, Italy (1982)

By the late 1970s it was clear that a second College on the continent of Europe was a priority if the movement was to retain its European credentials. The Atlantic College was known in Rome, thanks to the 1971 visit of a young diplomat from the London Embassy who had visited and reported enthusiastically. It took however over ten years before this College, the first to owe its birth and continuing existence entirely to governmental action (the Ministry of Foreign Affairs in Rome and the Regional Government of Friuli-Venezia Giulia) was opened. The College broke new ground by having a village, Duino, as its campus. Its focus from the start and the principal motivation for continuing governmental support has been its commitment to East–West integration, about a third of the students coming from Central and Eastern Europe by 1990.

Li Po Chun United World College of Hong Kong (1992)

Stimulated – one might almost say provoked – by fumbling attempts in the late 1980s to create a College on a university campus in China, Q. W. Lee, a prominent Hong Kong banker and leading figure in local education, swiftly arranged for a large and as yet undirected legacy to be applied to the foundation of this stepping stone to the emerging giant next door – a dozen of whose young people, many of them Red Guards in the Cultural Revolution, had been the first students from communist China ever to enter a western school, Atlantic College, in 1974. The links between Li Po Chun College and China are now strong, with all students undertaking social services projects there in their first year. The College has also been fostering an intriguing relationship of immense potential significance with North Korea.

Red Cross Nordic United World College, Norway (1995)

The leadership in the founding of this College lay almost entirely with a dedicated former student of the Atlantic College. Lying in spectacularly beautiful country in western Norway, its partnership with the Norwegian Red Cross (the campus is a shared facility) has encouraged the enrolment of disabled students and a special emphasis on work with disabled people not only in Norway, and not only in term time, through its community service activities. Like the Adriatic College, it is sponsored by the national and other governmental authorities.

Mahindra United World College of India, near Pune (1997)

The first serious attempts to found a College in India were, naturally enough, strongly encouraged in the very early 1970s by the then UWC President and former Viceroy of India, Lord Mountbatten. Sites were found and budgets prepared, but not even he could persuade Prime Minister Indira Gandhi to authorise the project. It was only when the industrialist Harish Mahindra entered the scene that the vision became a reality. Cooperation with the neighbouring villages is the keynote of the community service. Thanks to Akshara (the Access to Opportunities project), over a hundred students in grades 8 to 10 of the local high school are given additional educational support each year by the College. This initiative has enabled many local young people to enter Indian or American universities and vocational training schemes that had previously been beyond their reach.

United World College in Mostar, Bosnia and Herzegovina (2006)

The so-called UWC–IB initiative has been a natural continuation of the commitment of the Adriatic College to Central and Eastern Europe. The College in Mostar is the first to have been inserted directly into the buildings and structure of a national system. Virtually all state schools in the critically divided country of Bosnia and Herzegovina are segregated between the Muslim Bosniak, Catholic Croat and Orthodox Serb communities. The College aims to establish a model for international education in post-conflict societies. An integral part of the initiative is the programme for the professional development of teachers from across the country with workshops, conferences and study visits, especially to Slovenia.

This college was originally set up in 2006 for a three-year experimental period but continues to survive against the financial odds.

United World College of Costa Rica (2006)

UWC Costa Rica was formerly the SOS International College Hermann Gmeiner Costa Rica, a project of the SOS Children's Villages organisation. It is the first in the UWC movement to operate fully as a bilingual school. Some students take their IB diploma in English, some in Spanish, and others register for the bilingual diploma. The College is committed to the annual enrolment of pupils from SOS. Some 40–50% of the students come from Latin America and the Caribbean.

UNITED WORLD COLLEGES FOR ALL AGES

United World College of South East Asia, Singapore (1971)

It was at first hoped to establish a College offering two-year courses on the same lines as the Atlantic College. The exploratory work was done during the confrontation in the late 1960s between Malaysia, Indonesia and Singapore, and it was planned that all students would divide their time equally between campuses in the three countries. In the event, sixth-form scholarship students from other countries were carefully inserted into the existing international St John's School, run for the already significant international business community in Singapore. In stages the school evolved to become a full United World College. UWC SEA has a wider age range – 4 to 18 years – and a larger school population, now 3,500 pupils, than other members of the movement. A second campus opens in August 2011, bringing the student population to 5,000.

The College's Global Concerns Programme highlights global issues and enables students to become involved, often as leaders, in ambitious community service projects, chiefly across South East Asia. Their efforts contribute, for example, to the building of schools in Swaziland, Nepal and Aceh, Indonesia.

Waterford KaMhlaba United World College South Africa, Swaziland (1981)

This College was founded in 1963 by idealists from within South Africa who recognised the urgent need for an accessible alternative to the segregated education universal in their own schools. Its community of purpose with the Atlantic College crystallised when a Deputy Head from Waterford moved to the Atlantic College, and led to its enthusiastic enrolment in the UWC movement in 1981. Many South African people distinguished in the fight against apartheid entrusted their children to the College, among them Nelson Mandela, Archbishop Tutu and Nadime Gordimer.

The College's environment presents all the challenges of the developing world: the importance of education and of inter-racial understanding, poverty, and the devastating consequences of Aids and HIV in the neighbouring villages.

United World College Maastricht, The Netherlands (2009)

This College has arisen from the combined efforts of enthusiasts, principally UWC graduates, from The Netherlands, Belgium, Germany and Luxembourg. It embraces the International Department of Joppenhof Primary School and the International School of Maastricht and has some 500 pupils of more than 40 nationalities. Work on a new campus, including residential facilities, begins early in 2010. The Dutch Ministry of Education expects UWC Maastricht to become a role model for the integration of community service into Dutch state schools.

The United World College Vocational College

Simón Bolívar United World College of Venezuela (1988)

This College, a vocational post-secondary institute focusing on agricultural management in tropical climates, has been the movement's first and hitherto only attempt to tackle directly the environmental challenges of the developing world. Based on an early design for an apprentices' school in Thailand developed and advocated unsuccessfully by Desmond Hoare, it was to become The Prince of Wales' most distinctive contribution to the movement as he, jointly with the Venezuelan agronomist Luis Marcano, persuaded the President of Venezuela to give it his backing. Theoretical instruction is combined with practical, hands-on experience and extensive involvement in community-based rural development projects. After three years the successful students are awarded degrees in farm administration. The language of the College is Spanish.

THE UWC NATIONAL COMMITTEES

Aaland	Canada	Greece
Afghanistan	Cayman Islands	Greenland
Albania	Chile	Grenada
Algeria	China	Guatemala
Anguilla	Colombia	Guyana
Antigua and Barbuda	Congo Brazzaville	Haiti
Argentina	Costa Rica	Honduras
Australia	Croatia	Hong Kong SAR
Austria	Cuba	Hungary
Bahamas	Czech Republic	Iceland
Bahrain	Denmark	India
Bangladesh	Dominica	Indonesia
Barbados	Dominican Republic	Iran
Belarus	Ecuador	Iraq
Belgium	Egypt	Ireland
Belize	El Salvador	Israel
Benin	Eritrea	Italy
Bermuda	Estonia	Japan
Bhutan	Ethiopia	Jordan
Bolivia	Falkland Islands	Kenya
Bosnia and Herzegovina	Faroe Islands	Kosovo
Botswana	Fiji	Latvia
Brazil	Finland	Lebanon
Bulgaria	France	Lesotho
Burundi	Georgia	Libya
Cambodia	Germany	Lithuania
Cameroon	Ghana	Madagascar

Malawi	Peru	Sweden
Malaysia	Philippines	Switzerland
Maldives	Poland	Syria
Malta	Portugal	Taiwan
Mauritius	Qatar	Tanzania
Mexico	Romania	Thailand
Moldova	Russian Federation	Tibet
Mongolia	Rwanda	Timor-Leste
Montenegro	St Kitts and Nevis	Trinidad and Tobago
Montserrat	St Lucia	Tunisia
Morocco	St Vincent and The	Turkey
Mozambique	Grenadines	Turks & Caicos
Namibia	Saudi Arabia	UAE
Nepal	Senegal	Uganda
Netherlands	Serbia	UK
New Zealand	Sierra Leone	Ukraine
Nicaragua	Singapore	Uruguay
Nigeria	Slovakia	USA
Norway	South Africa	Venezuela
Oman	Spain	Vietnam
Pakistan	Sri Lanka	Western Sahara
Palestine	Sudan	Yemen
Panama	Suriname	Zambia
Paraguay	Swaziland	Zimbabwe

INTERNATIONAL BACCALAUREATE

The early origins of the IB may be found in documents from the 1920s that report on attempts in the fledgling International School of Geneva to create a school-leaving diploma across borders. Renewed attempts were made by the Conference of Internationally Minded Schools (CIS) in the 1950s. The ultimately decisive steps, commissioned by the International Schools Association, which had been founded in 1951, were taken by the staff of the International School of Geneva and the United Nations School of New York during the 1960s. The Atlantic College quickly allied itself with these pioneering efforts and became the project's showpiece in the United Kingdom (and perhaps further afield too) when it abandoned the traditional British GCE A-Levels in 1971 for this new curriculum and examination.

The IB diploma, which requires study over the last two years of secondary education, led in 1994 to the introduction of the Middle Years Programme and in 1997 to the Primary Years Programme. With these developments, both international and national schools were offered a curriculum covering the entire span of school attendance.

There are now (2010) 2,823 member schools of the IB worldwide, of which 2,066 offer the school-leaving and university-entry IB diploma.

Acknowledgements

There are innumerable quotations in this brief account. This is why they have been picked out in italics. To be truthful, almost the entire text should be in italics since it rests so heavily on an unashamed collection of extracts, chiefly from notes, letters and memoranda by Desmond Hoare, but also from articles in journals and addresses at conferences by others. Stanley Williams, the marine consultant and author of detailed professional summaries of the history of the rigid inflatable, will recognise many parts of the text, but I hope he will forgive me for indicating that he often cited Desmond Hoare word for word when reviewing the development of these boats.

Thanks then to all of these people, named and unnamed: to HRH the Duke of Edinburgh for allowing me to quote from his letter of 21st April 1964; to former and present colleagues at the College, especially Vicky Phillips and Gareth Rees; to officials of the RNLI who have helped me greatly; to the Secretary of the Royal Institution of Naval Architects who kindly made an expensive publication available to me free of charge; to Sip Wiebenga of the Dutch Life Saving Society (KNRM); to Maurice Bloomfield, who was with the film team who made that fine film *A Place in the World* in 1968, for the use of his photographs; to Tony Besse for all his interest, encouragement and negotiation with the Cousteau Foundation for photographs; and to the many former Atlantic College students who responded so willingly (many, I concede, a very long time ago), to my requests for anecdotes and memories. Chief among these must be Paul Jefferies (AC 1966–8), whose e-mailed advice and detailed comments from his home-built and round-the-world yacht off Australia have been invaluable; David Nockels (AC 1969–71) for his piece on the BP developments; Reynier Overhoff from The Netherlands (AC 1969–71), who gave his former Headmaster a stern ticking-off for failing to complete his homework in timely fashion; Otto van Voorst (AC 1967–9), also from The Netherlands, one of the two student builders of *Psychedelic Surfer*; and Willem de Vogel, likewise Dutch (AC 1967–9) and the other builder of *Psychedelic Surfer* (the Dutch are everywhere in the story), who through his financial assistance with the publication of this account has made it possible for income from sales to go to the Atlantic College's Scholarship Fund.

This is not, I must emphasise, a balanced review of College life in the early years. It says very little about the remarkable teaching of those pioneering colleagues and their immediate successors, or of the really noteworthy accomplishments in drama and art – unforgettable, at least for me, are Meurig Owen's *Murder in the Cathedral* and *Doctor Faustus* (the devils in Naomi Hoare skin suits with forked tails) in the College dining hall, and the results achieved by Charles and Mary White in the art and pottery departments. Nor is there any acknowledgement of those students who found the whole thing rather breezy and 'naval' – and one must remember that, unlike the traditional public school clientele, the students were away from home for the first time in their lives, unconditioned by prep or public school and family tradition. Their reactions were all part of the creative mix and had an important place in College life.

In correspondence some years ago with George Cooper, a former Chief Inspector with the RNLI, I floated the vague idea of using this account as a fundraiser. The word in my letter was mistyped as 'funraiser'. I am not sure that it will have been fun to read, but it has been fun to write. Nothing can however compare with the sheer enjoyment and sense of pride in having been a modest observer and participant as all these developments took place. These sentiments are only strengthened by the kindness of Naomi Hoare in contributing the Foreword.

Picture Acknowledgements

All illustrations are from the archives of Atlantic College with some notable exceptions listed below. Many fine photographs in the early years of Atlantic College were taken by Dr. Bill Evans of Bridgend, the father of two College students. Desmond Hoare was himself an enthusiastic and successful photographer. Many of their pictures appear in this book and are acknowledged. The author and publisher would also like to thank the British Royal National Lifeboat Institution and the Dutch KNRM for their assistance and support in the supply of images. Finally, the author and publisher would like to acknowledge the photographs that were taken by students or individuals whom we have been unable to contact; apologies are offered to anyone to whom it has not been possible to give a full credit.

The Associated Press, p. 35 (left); Herbie Barnes, p. 32 (top left); Paul Barrett, pp. 9, 110 (top); W.H. Bartlett, p. 7; Maurice Bloomfield, pp. 50, 61, 62-3 (far left, lower centre left, centre, centre right), 66; The Cousteau Society, pp. 22–3 (main, far left); Crown Copyright, p. 106; Dr. Bill Evans, pp. 2, 10, 11, 16 (top), 18, 19, 20; the family of Desmond Hoare, pp. 4, 16 (bottom); Desmond Hoare, pp. inside back flap, vii, 12, 38, 43, 46, 56, 58–9, 76–7, 79, 87, 109 (main), 114; Tim Jaques for the Goring Hotel, London, p. 69 (top right); Paul Jefferies and Martti Salomaa, pp. 34, 51 (top); the Jigsaw Project, pp. 93, 94, 96; Keystone Press, pp. 14, 115; KNRM pp. 100, 104; KNRM/Arie van Dijk, front cover (main), 128; KNRM/ Heert Jan van Keulen, p. 101 (top); KNRM /Timco Haukema, pp. 101 (bottom), 105; KNRM/Jan Willem Wolf, p. 102; KNRM/Janneke Stokroos, p. 103; *Life International* magazine, p. 39; National Maritime Museum, p. 21; Royal National Lifeboat Institution, pp. 26–7, 89, 91; Salem School Archive, p. 3; Jenny Slack, p. 122; South Wales Echo, p. 118; Dennis Stephens, p. 45 (right); David Sutcliffe, pp. endpapers, 1, 63 (far right); J.S. Templeton, p. 8; United States Navy/Kristopher Wilson, p. 125; Western Mail & Echo Ltd, pp. 17 (bottom), 35 (right), 45 (left).

Index